PENGUIN BOOKS

iPARENT: EMBRACING PARENTING IN THE DIGITAL AGE

Neha J Hiranandani has spent the last two decades working on development issues, with a focus on gender equity in various organizations, including the United Nations. She completed her undergraduate degree with honors in international relations and English literature from Wellesley College, and has a master's in education policy from Harvard University.

Neha's columns on social and economic issues have appeared in several prominent publications, including *Indian Express*, Huffington Post, NDTV and *Vogue*. Her first book, *Girl Power! Indian Women Who Broke the Rules*, was a national bestseller.

Celebrating 35 Years of
Penguin Random House India

ADVANCE PRAISE FOR THE BOOK

'An insightful portrayal of the dynamics between modern parenting and technology, this book should be read by every parent trying to navigate the digital landscape'—Sonali Bendre, actor

'Realizing in her own home that "more devices than people live here", and that parenting today involves dealing with challenges that no previous generation has ever encountered, Neha J Hiranandani has written an invaluable guide to coping with the complexities of raising kids in a brave new world. Laced with insight, empathy, humour and broad-mindedness, *iParent* is a must-read for any parent!'—Dr Shashi Tharoor, Indian parliamentarian, writer and former UN Under Secretary General

'A humorous and revealing introduction to the Internet as iGen sees it. With an astute blend of wit and wisdom, this is a wake-up call that educates as it entertains. An indispensable guide for parenting in the modern age'—Anand Mahindra, non-executive chairperson, Mahindra Group

'Both intimate and broad, *iParent* is a spirited account of how being online changes how we live and love. Don't let it pass you by!'—Shekhar Kapur, award-winning film-maker

'Eye-opening, insightful and funny, Neha J Hiranandani has written the new handbook for parents traversing the technological landscape. More than answers, she points us to the questions we should be asking—and how we might reframe them to imagine the future' —Avni Doshi, Booker-shortlisted author of *Girl in White Cotton*

iParent

Embracing Parenting in the Digital Age

Neha J Hiranandani

PENGUIN BOOKS

An imprint of Penguin Random House

PENGUIN BOOKS

USA | Canada | UK | Ireland | Australia
New Zealand | India | South Africa | China | Singapore

Penguin Books is part of the Penguin Random House group of companies
whose addresses can be found at global.penguinrandomhouse.com

Published by Penguin Random House India Pvt. Ltd
4th Floor, Capital Tower 1, MG Road,
Gurugram 122 002, Haryana, India

First published in Penguin Books by Penguin Random House India 2023

10 9 8 7 6 5 4 3 2 1

ISBN   9780143449744

Typeset in Sabon by MAP Systems, Bengaluru, India
Printed at

www.penguin.co.in

for Zoya, my life
and
for Jahan, my world

Contents

Contents

Introduction

Zoya, my eleven-year-old, has been asked to give a speech at the school assembly dressed as an important character from history. Their class is hosting 'A Night at the Museum' event, and the kids are researching important people that changed the tide of humanity—essentially museum-worthy folks. I ask Zoya what the popular characters are, expecting to see several Mother Teresas and a bunch of M.K. Gandhis. 'Not really, mom. A lot of people are dressing up as MrBeast this year,' she replies. Move over Margaret Thatcher and Barack Obama, there's a new kid in town: Jimmy Donaldson aka MrBeast is one of the world's most popular YouTubers. In a video that went mega-viral, MrBeast sits in one place until he counts to 1,00,000—a feat that took him over forty hours. Apparently, that's now considered museum-worthy. Someone should tell the folks at Madame Tussauds.

Perhaps I shouldn't be so shocked at this new world order. Looking around my house, it quickly becomes apparent that more devices than people live here. Both my children are digital natives for whom the idea of living without technology inspires incredulity. On a recent Saturday evening, Zoya asked me to email her teacher. I sent the email but pointed out that this idea of being connected with everyone all the time is relatively new. 'Growing up, we didn't have email and if I wanted to talk to my teacher on the weekend, I had to wait until Monday,' I told her. 'You didn't have email?' asked Zoya, her brown eyes growing wider with disbelief. 'But then, how did you send someone a message?' And before I could respond, she earnestly answered her question. 'Wait, wait. I know what you would have done! You would have sent pigeons.'

Pigeons?

Pigeons!

They think we sent each other messages tied to pigeons!

Our kids are iGen—digital natives, born with a phone in one hand and a tablet in the other—and for them technology is so ubiquitous that a time without it is positively medieval! Most of them were handed a device before they could walk; they clicked and scrolled before they took their first bite, tapped and dragged before they said their first words. With every move posted online, their digital footprints follow them like live locations from platform to platform, pinging and beeping as they navigate this web. It's as though humanity has moved to a different planet in a single generation.

Growing up, my parents had a simple mantra for my sister and me when we left the house: 'Be home before dark and don't leave the colony'. But today, deadlines and *laxman rekhas* seem pointless when iGen can circle the globe in seconds. I would sometimes bump into the neighbourhood cutie on those walks with my sister, a phenomenon that merited an excited diary entry. 'KEEP OUT! PRIVATE!' I would emblazon across my secret diary to keep my thoughts away from my parents' prying eyes. But secret diary entries about neighbourhood crushes seem trivial when we realize that our kids can create entire worlds online and invent new personas that we can never access. Teenagers have long been accused of being 'in their own world' by bewildered parents, and no phrase could be more accurate for iGen that hangs out in this boundless, borderless playground even as they sit beside us in the same living room. This book is an exploration of those worlds as they unfold. In fact, it's an attempt to join the kids in their web. Some of the findings are surprising, and others are disturbing but rest assured, that it's not all bad.

Technology offers our kids vast advantages as they bypass borders, collaborate with people around the world and learn the languages of countries that we struggle to place on a map. They can engage in discussions around body positivity and gender neutrality—concepts that parents don't always know and that schools often forget to teach. As they surf these digital waves, being online provides many in iGen with an escape hatch where they won't get body-shamed, teased about acne marks or have classmates mimic their stutter. It's pretty darn liberating. Last New Year's Eve (NYE), I walked into a party and jigged alongside a gorilla in a tuxedo, a leopard in a hot pink bikini and a chef with a unicorn horn. Gorilla, leopard, unicorn and I had similar ideas to skip the maddening traffic on NYE and so, we chose to party on VRChat, a popular virtual reality platform. While I was there, I got talking to one of the other partygoers, a sort of cross between a rabbit and Wonder Woman, named NikNot who had recently joined the platform's thriving LGBTQIA+ community. 'My family is very conservative and if it wasn't for VR, I wouldn't have been able to celebrate New Year's as myself,' she said. I looked around the party and saw her point. For the leopard in the bikini, VR allows you to be who you want to be. For the queer kid coming out of the closet, it allows you to be who you are.

It's not just the kids—technology often makes life better for all of us. During Covid, we went from spending time online to quite literally, living digitally. My phone became a conduit for life itself. A few days into Lockdown 1, my cousin gave birth to a baby boy. The baby's first meeting with his extended family was watching his grandparents, uncles and aunts coo at him from little Zoom squares. A few minutes into the Zoom call, the new mother had to step away because she had a video consult scheduled with her gynaecologist. She undressed and the doctor went on to examine her perineum on WhatsApp video. Let that sink in for a moment. In fact, there was a lot that sank in that year. Covid relentlessly marched on and when Diwali arrived, we gathered around our laptops to light virtual *diyas* with the scattered family. No one seemed perturbed as we performed the digital puja—even the baby had become used to living, learning and loving online. As it neared Christmas, my dad's schoolmates connected on a Facebook group and organized a Zoom reunion.

All firmly in their seventies, old school buddies peered at their screens and lifted their glasses to see—many for the first time—what their best friend from school looks like now. Watching those little squares join one another and listening to the inevitable jokes about bald patches and wrinkles, I marvelled at how tech had connected us all. In the months that followed, both celebrations and cremations took place with friends and family attending in pixels. By then, several tech companies had consolidated their positions as the richest businesses in the history of the world. In fact, when the *Financial Times* released a list of the top companies that profited from the pandemic,[1] it was unsurprising that ten out of ten from the 'Top 10' were tech companies. And when Elon Musk went shopping for Twitter, he further emphasized the point that we've all understood: in the new world order, only tech companies are formidable enough to compete with other tech companies.

But parenting in this new world order comes with high stakes. 'We're sort of in the midst of a natural kind of uncontrolled experiment on the next generation of children,'[2] says Dr Christakis from the American Academy of Paediatrics. This *uncontrolled experiment* dwarfs anything that humans have ever experienced. The world has over fifteen billion connected devices, almost double the number of people on Earth. Closer home, more than half a billion Indians are now connected to the Internet—posting, learning and loving—making India one of the world's fastest-growing online markets. But no matter how out of control this experiment might seem, it's impossible for any parent to completely abandon tech. In fact, tech has never been as central to our children's lives. Pre-Covid, 45 per cent of American teens admitted to being online 'almost constantly' and the numbers in Indian metros were similar. Covid took the other half of kids who weren't 'almost constantly' online and propelled them straight into the digital world. Reports suggest[3] that children's screen time has doubled, perhaps even tripled post pandemic. I called a friend who had worked hard to keep her nine-year-old away from devices. 'Yeah, that's all gone now,' she said, 'everyone is at the party.'

Everyone really is at the party. But being at this party is challenging everything that humanity has ever known about anything including our bodies. Dr D.K., a leading ophthalmologist, tells me that eye conditions that were rare just ten years ago are becoming increasingly common today. 'It used to be very unusual to find a myopic pre-schooler but now, I see a few myopic toddlers a week. Our eyes are evolving to only see things that are right in front of us,' she says, stretching out her hand as though she was holding a phone. With the metaverse knocking at our door, it is evident that tech has changed our biology, our physiology and now underpins every issue in the world from whom we choose as prime minister to what we find sexy.

But how do we deal with our kids being subjects of an uncontrolled experiment? Unfortunately, kids don't come with instruction manuals (I checked at the hospital a couple of times!) and when faced with the daunting prospect of raising a human, most of us usually turn to older generations for advice. *How did you do it*? we ask the hands that so lovingly raised us. When my daughter was ready to start eating solids, I instinctively called my grandmother. For the next half hour, she painstakingly explained her recipes and so my daughter's first meal was filled with ghee, *gur* and *badi nani's* wisdom. Generations before us have reached out to the village when bringing up a child—it's a natural reflex. But today, as we raise kids in this digital age, the village disappears. For the first time, there is no recipe to follow, no guidebook to consult and no traditional wisdom to rely upon. Asking your mother for advice when your kid is being cyberbullied or gathering her thoughts on sexting is pointless because neither she nor anyone in her generation has parented like this. In fact, not only is there no guidebook on this, but we also don't even know what 'this' really is. Sure, human beings have always invented things—the wheel, the telephone, vaccines and the printing press (thanks to which I have a job!). But there is no precedent in human history for the impact of the Internet and so, we—kids *and parents alike*—are the experiment.

How do we navigate this uncertain future that includes cyberbullying, sexting and the overuse of social media— each issue a potential minefield? What do these worlds look like? Who are the kids meeting in the metaverse? How are they learning? How about falling in love? Is cybersex real sex? And cyberbullying—is that real too? Talking about tech with kids from every corner of the country, this book explores the digital playground where our children make friends, negotiate conflicts and discover love. Most of us will admit that our kids know far more about tech than we do as adults. Is there any point in voicing our opinion when we, as parents, are on the wrong side of the digital divide? I would argue that there is. Medieval or not, we are the last generation to remember phones that plugged into walls instead of supercomputers that slide into pockets. And if we are the last of humanity to know what life was like without the Internet, it seems to me that we should share those stories. Maybe there is something to be learned from the old tales, like Goldilocks, who suggested that things should neither be too hot nor too cold. She taught us that the temperature of the porridge must be just right, and the strategies in this book detail how we might strike that balance. Ultimately, the recipe for your family's porridge will be your own, seasoned to your taste and adjusted to your family's preference. Eating is the one thing you can't do online and so this is an invitation for us to put the phones away and cook together. Bon appétit.

CHAPTER ONE

THE GREAT DIGITAL DIVIDE

As an average parent in your thirties or forties, you likely use three social media platforms: Facebook, Instagram and Twitter. Perhaps you downloaded Snapchat after taking a Buzzfeed quiz to determine your mental age. In an adventurous moment, you've made a few TikTok videos all of which made your kids laugh hysterically. (That hurtful, 'I'm laughing *at* you, not *with* you' kind of mirth.) If you are like me, perhaps you hung out on the now-defunct Houseparty app during Lockdown 1 and awkwardly held a drink while pretending not to be enveloped by an impending sense of global doom. At the peak of pandemic boredom, you might have made a few Instagram reels to see what the fuss is about. And of course, you and I are now certifiable Zoom maestros. On a good day, while properly caffeinated, we can change Zoom backgrounds, turn off videos, share screens and even set up a waiting room. We've mastered the online game, right?

Wrong! The kids don't live here anymore. Discord, GroupMe, Kik Messenger and Whisper are some of the wildly popular sites on which tweens and teens live their daily lives; these are the playgrounds where romances bloom, hearts break, and the teen hunger games are won and lost. It's not an accident that you haven't heard about them because frankly if either you or I made our way on to these platforms, the kids would leave. That's what happened to Facebook a few years ago: as soon as the uncles and aunties decided to join Facebook, the kids fled the scene.[1] 'My mom joining FB totally killed the vibe,' says Ishaan, nineteen. 'She keeps sending me friend requests.' Ishaan still has a Facebook account but doesn't consider himself an active user. 'Anything

I post on FB will be seen by my whole family, so I don't post anything there anymore,' he says. Like most other kids, he has a 'Finsta' on Instagram, essentially an account with a cryptic unidentifiable handle where he posts 'the real stuff'. I hate to break it to you but if you think you're following your kid on Insta, there's a good chance that you're following the wrong account.

Now that we're talking Finstas, we may as well be done with the bad news: there is a definitive digital divide between generations, something we make glaringly obvious when we ask our kids to pause their online game! But park the jokes and it becomes obvious that the divide is real and it's virtually unbridgeable. Several times a week, I hand my phone to a kid half my age to fix a setting, find out why AirDrop isn't working or figure out a new app. 'When Aanya starts talking about Roblox, I have to tell her, "*Beta*, I literally don't understand a word that's coming out of your mouth,"' laughs my friend about her ten-year-old daughter. During the pandemic, my friend Viraj wanted to make an iMovie to celebrate his dad's seventieth birthday. 'Since we couldn't celebrate together, I asked the whole family to send in messages and I thought I'll make a nice video for Dad. But learning to use iMovie was tough—it was taking me days!' he says. Viraj's eight-year-old daughter Siya watched her father flounder before asking him to move over. 'She finished the whole thing in a couple of hours! This kid had never used iMovie before, and she leapfrogged me in minutes. She's a pro!' Viraj gushes. I can literally see Siya roll her eyes at her dad's exclamations because here's the thing: Siya isn't really a pro, she's just a digital native. Tech is her first language, her 'mother tongue' if you will. Siya, like many of our children, belongs to iGen, a generation that is growing up almost entirely online, subjects in a massive global experiment with no control group.

But if our children are digital natives, what does that make us? Well, immigrants. (I told you we were getting ahead of the bad news here.) Experts say the human brain has the best chance of learning a new language before the age of ten and technology came to us well after that age. It will forever be our second language,* and we will always be the fumbling, clumsy immigrants speaking with funny accents and trying to keep up. Recently my daughter Zoya asked me what I knew about ships. Surprised at my kid's sudden nautical interest, I started to mumble something about masts and anchors while she giggled at her blathering mother. "Not *those* ships, Mom," she laughed. You know, *ships*!" But I didn't know. For me, ships were water cars, and I had no idea that dictionary.com had updated its definition of 'ship' to this:

> *verb*
>
> to take an interest in or hope for a romantic
> relationship between (fictional characters or

---

* Here's a roundup of some phrases you should know in your second language:
- 'Fire' is something amazing. As in, 'that vine is fire.'
- 'Shade' is an insult. It is usually thrown. As in, 'the teacher just threw shade at me for not doing my homework.'
- 'Gucci' is not your handbag. Or your shoes. Or even your jacket. Gucci is something good. As in, 'can you come over now? That'll be Gucci.'
- 'ELI5' means Explain Like I'm 5. Which is how my tween explains most things to me. Now you know. And IYKYK.

famous people), whether or not the romance actually exists: *I'm shipping for those guys—they would make a great couple*!

When did 'ship' go from being a noun to a verb?

Of course, every group has some cool kids and even in our limping immigrant group, there will be some who got the memo about the new ship. I've spoken to dozens of grandmothers who make hot Instagram reels, dads who play *Fortnite* with their kids and middle-aged influencers who make a living by plying their wares online. But even if you are on the right side of the digital divide today, this will likely not remain an immutable truth tomorrow. Unlike us immigrants who tend to balance digital with analogue, our kids are living virtually every part of their lives online. While we exchange WhatsApp numbers with a new friend, iGen exchanges gaming handles so they can meet their new friend in an alternate reality. And so, with every passing day, *we get more plugged out while the natives get more plugged in*. We can install parental controls, place restrictions on content and adjust privacy settings until our fingers fall off but much of this will end up as misguided attempts to outrun natives on their home turf. Graham Clark, the mastermind who hacked Twitter in March 2020, was just seventeen years old.[2] Clark held the Twitter accounts of Barack Obama and Jeff Bezos hostage before he was legally allowed to hold a beer. Another teenager recently found a flaw in Tesla's security system allowing him to access Tesla vehicles in thirteen countries including opening doors and disabling the cars' security features![3] Now, while it is unlikely that our kids are hacking Twitter or exposing Tesla, it is probable that they are playing video games with folks from all over the globe, trading 'skins' and crypto while we're still puzzling over how to change display pics on Instagram.

Just like we devised ways to outsmart our parents, this generation is doing the same. In a recent survey, 64 per cent of Indian children said that they know how to hide their online activity from their parents. 'I always keep one safe tab open—like schoolwork—so I can quickly switch to it if needed,' says Rashi, fifteen. 'And then I can also quickly type POS (Parent Over Shoulder) or 9 (code for POS) that red-alerts everyone that my parents are in the room.' Incidentally, I asked Rashi if there is a code for when parents leave the room. There is. It's 99. You're welcome.

'Did you find dad on Amazon?'

Covid brought this digital divide between generations into sharp focus. Toddlers and pre-schoolers were the 'lockdown kids' for whom life became a carousel of online classes, virtual playdates, video calls with grandparents and online orders. My five-year-old son Jahan is a product of these circumstances having spent more than half his life in lockdown. Until recently, he had no memories of going to a physical store and thought that Amazon was a giant shop in the cloud (mostly true) that could deliver anything from toys to toothbrushes (also true). 'Did you find dad on Amazon?' he asked one afternoon while I was online shopping. My eyes opened as wide as the saucers that I was trying to order. His father and I met at a Big Fat Indian wedding but every wedding that Jahan has ever attended has been on Zoom.

Often because iGen hasn't experienced as much of the same thing IRL (in real life), they are more willing to accept the digital alternative. A Zoom wedding instead of the real deal. Browsing online instead of going to a bookstore. Playing video games instead of getting your hands dirty in the playground. With limited exposure to a truly offline world, they are most receptive to the immersive charms of the digital, remaining ever happy to browse, love and party online. With the arrival of the metaverse, their online life is set to get more immersive than ever. Within the last decade, the Internet has already gone from visual to interactive and the next step promises to revolutionize humanity's relationship with digital environments. No one can predict what shape this relationship will ultimately take; that would be like sitting in 1990 and trying to predict today's Internet. But the future is knocking on our doors—Apple has released the Vision Pro and Zuckerberg continues to promise that the metaverse will be spectacular. Think of the metaverse as an 'embodied internet where you're in the experience, not just looking at it,'[4] he says. Apologies to Zuckerberg but I think my grandmother said it better. I was explaining the idea of the metaverse to her and expected her to have some difficulty grasping the details. She got it within seconds. '*Aakhir hum phone he andar ghus hi gaye!*' she said. Mic drop.

And lest we dismiss Internet 3.0 as irrelevant, it's worth remembering that this isn't some niche network designed for nerds in dusty basements; the makers of

Facebook are aiming at making the metaverse central to the lives of billions across the globe. Everyone is invited to Zuckerberg's global metaverse party and it's no surprise that the kids are among the first to arrive and the last to leave.

I decided to bite the bullet and tried out Meta Quest 2, currently one of the more popular ways to have an immersive metaverse experience. The Meta Quest 2 is clunky, but Meta's ambition is to condense this gadget to a pair of lightweight eyeglasses that fit in your pocket. Put on the glasses and you can instantly sit in the front row at Adele's concert or have dinner with your friends on the other side of the planet. I wanted to know if snowboarding from my kitchen or hiking up Mount Vesuvius from my living room was worth the trip but since my workout game wasn't fiery enough to be done atop an active volcano, I opted for a leisurely African safari instead. I strapped on the headset and instantly felt disoriented. But the awkwardness quickly disappeared as I watched the orange sun setting across the dappled Serengeti while a herd of zebras trampled past me, noisily snorting dust from their nostrils. Walking a little further, I almost tripped over a pride of lions yawning under a thorny acacia tree. I sat down to watch them and only when my posterior hit the carpet did I remember that I was in my bedroom in Delhi, the view from which was tangled electric wires, a pooping pigeon* and endless smog. This metaverse thing was cool!

I can see how many things will be easier in the metaverse. Imagine standing in the middle of the solar system and gazing around as the Milky Way slowly

---

* I should note that this was not a carrier pigeon as imagined by iGen.

unfolds around you. That seems like a much better way to learn about the wonders of the galaxy than some static illustration in a science textbook. Decades ago, my high school physics teacher tried to explain refraction by holding up an object saying, 'This is a glass made of glass.' He immediately stopped in embarrassment as the class erupted in laughter. Later that month, most of us took our physics exams not knowing much more about refraction than that single evergreen sentence. While 'glass made of glass' has been memorialized and repeated with glee at every school reunion, it didn't do much to explain how light bends. Think of standing in the middle of a room as countless prisms stretch out in every direction creating twisting rainbows of light as you watch science in action—that's how physics can be taught in the metaverse.

Mega in the Meta

Although he isn't learning physics, Ishaan spends more time on Sandbox, a booming metaverse, than on any other social media platform on Internet 2.0. He recently managed to get an invite to Snoop Dogg's exclusive metaverse party where he hung out with the rapper. Or rather, his avatar breathed the same digital air as Snoop's avatar. 'My life's biggest regret is not being able to buy the land next to Snoop's.* He has the hottest parties and for the most exclusive ones, he only invites his neighbours,' says Ishaan.

But it's not just about physics and parties, the metaverse also means profit. I speak to Harsheen who

---

* Someone paid $450,000 to be Snoop's neighbour in the metaverse.

has a booming metaverse business. Harsheen's avatar was entering a club—in the metaverse—when the bouncer stopped her because she was wearing sneakers. 'That was when I had the idea to set up a shoe shop right next to the club!' says Harsheen, who is inspired by brands such as Gucci, Louis Vuitton and Forever 21, all of which have big metaverse retail presence. They are mega in the meta. A friend, Garima, was amazed when her son asked for a quarter of the popular cryptocurrency Ethereum for his fifteenth birthday. 'Did you give it to him?' I asked. 'I wish I had!' she replied. 'He trades NFTs in the metaverse and wanted to buy a particular skin with the Ethereum. That skin has now tripled in value. He would have made so much money if I had given it to him!' Not to be left behind, my five-year-old's nursery classmate recently asked for his birthday presents to all be in Robux.

Whether it's the metaverse or the regular Internet 2.0, our children's first playground will likely be online. During Covid, they met new teachers and classmates online for the first time and had their 'first day of class' jitters with rows of squares set on a screen. Willingly or not, we have given this the all-important parental seal of approval and, therefore, meeting someone new online is now unlikely to ring alarm bells for our kids. Just as we used to run into our neighbourhood park looking for our playmates, they enter this digital playground scanning the scene for connections, comments and likes. None of it needs to stay in the safety of the neighbourhood and in fact, online worlds are the perfect place to indulge in impulsive, risk-taking behaviour long considered the hallmark of the teenage mind. While you can hope that your child is only going online to study the solar system, the reality is likely to be different. It promises to be a mixed bag.

iGen is experiencing record levels of depression, anxiety and body image issues. Doctors around the world are flagging it as a tsunami of mental health problems. Much of the toxic baggage of the 'old Internet' will indisputably make its way into the metaverse while new problems will likely be exacerbated. The metaverse is already facing harassment and groping issues[5] and experts warn that mixing kids and adult strangers in a self-moderated virtual world will create unprecedented opportunities for sexual predators. Who is going to regulate things in the metaverse? Nina Patel says she was sexually assaulted within a minute of entering the metaverse. 'They essentially, but virtually, gang-raped my avatar and took photos as I tried to get away,' she says.[6] This presents a sobering reality check: as the Internet continues to evolve, we will have to parent our children in a world that we can barely understand ourselves.

But here's the thing, it isn't about keeping up (that's quite impossible anyway). We don't have to know every platform or every phrase that iGen is using. Neither do we have to be tech moguls or metaverse experts. As parents, our first job will be to teach them digital hygiene and how to pull emergency brakes if the situation spins uncontrollably. We just have to be woke enough so that they don't have to ELI5. That way, they won't be able to throw shade at us and IMHO, that's pretty Gucci.

CHAPTER TWO

THROUGH THE LOOKING GLASS:
PEERING INTO SOCIAL
MEDIA'S MIRROR

Dope, Baby, Dope

It's that delicious week between Christmas and New Year's Eve when everyone is sparkling. I'm dressed for dinner and decide to pause for a photo by the tree which by some Christmas miracle turns out to be a bomb photo! You know the one—that turbocharged picture that gets more likes in an hour than the limping others get all day. Sure enough, within minutes of posting, the fire emojis start dropping, followed by the most delicious comments. 'Looking great!', 'Hot stuff', 'Love ittttt!!!!' The comments fill me up and I spend most of the car ride to dinner glued to my phone, ignoring my friends and questioning why I'm not more active on Insta. 'I really should post more,' I tell myself giddily.

That night, the champagne is being served in the most gorgeous Baccarat flutes. But who needs bubbly when you can drink dopamine? I spend more time checking my Insta notifications than I do talking to anyone around me—suddenly, my friends don't sparkle anymore. In fact, they seem positively dull compared to what's happening online. My Insta is on fire, so I decide to take another photograph for my story. I set the champagne flute next to my calligraphed place card and adjust the crystal teardrop candles so that the frame is prettily clustered in that exact Insta way. A few feet away, another woman seems to be doing the same thing. I check her story and sure enough, there's an impossibly glamorous shot of the same table. I look at my photo which seems so staged in comparison. This sucks. But whatever! I dive back into my DMs and read all the comments on my Christmas tree photo again. I'm feeling pretty buzzed when I realize that I haven't even sipped my champagne.

I'm drunk on dopamine.

The Siren Call of the Cellphone

Reports suggest that the average person checks their phone twelve times an hour. Many of these checks are almost Pavlovian in nature: where's my phone? Let me check my phone. Ok, I've checked my WhatsApp. Good. Hang on, is my phone buzzing? Must check the phone. Wait, I think I've lost my phone. I'll die if I lose my phone. Oh, thank God, here's my phone. I found my phone. Let me check my phone.

Even when we meet IRL, our conversations often revolve around our phones. 'Omg, which filter is that?', 'When did she post that update?', 'He looks so cute in that photo.' Essentially, we're either on our phones or talking about them. A study of US college students revealed that 60 per cent of them report being addicted to their phones.[1] I'm on a Zoom call with a group of college students from Chennai, and I ask them what they think of that statistic. It doesn't surprise them—they can't seem to get off their phones either:

'The phone pulls you in.'

'I keep checking my phone—I can't stop.'

'When I wake up in the morning, the first thing I check is my phone. It's always there, waiting for me.'

Ask any psychologist. That's the language of addiction. It's dopamine-drunk talk.

At its simplest, dopamine is a feel-good neurochemical released by the brain when you do something enjoyable, like taking a bite of cake, doing a killer workout or having sex. Because it feels *so damn good,* it makes you want to go back and do the thing again. You reach for one more bite, one more gym session, another round of shaking the sheets. From an evolutionary perspective, being wired this way makes perfect sense since food, fitness and getting your freak on are key to sustaining the human species. And yet, if I asked you to tell me something that you *have to do* every single day, you would likely include checking your phone. Not just once but multiple times. You might forget to eat, the gym membership might elapse, and you might become a poster child for abstinence, but you won't forget to check your phone. How is it that our phones have become more important than the biological acts that keep us alive? Here's a clue: it's not by accident, it's by design.

Big Tech has discovered that the most reliable way to keep you hooked is to simply hack your neural circuitry to release dopamine on cue. When you get a heart on your Instagram photo, a like on your Facebook post, or even the ping of a new WhatsApp notification, your brain releases dopamine in response to these 'digital rewards'. Once you've tasted the dopamine hit of a like or an emoji, you're hooked. You're stuck in a compulsion loop best described by the Pepsi slogan from the 1990s: *dil maange more.*[*] And as your brain adapts to the stimulus, you enter a dopamine deficit state that makes you seek more dopamine to get high. This will be all too familiar if you've ever tried alcohol: at first, a couple of sips were enough to make you stumble, but soon you needed the entire peg to feel the same rush. *Dil maange more.*

Virtually every successful product—the Coke recipe, the Google algorithm, my nani's rajma chawal—has a trade secret, a closely guarded ingredient critical to product success. For social media companies, *dopamine is that secret sauce*; it's the Kim Kardashian of molecules,[2] the ingredient that makes the apps stick and dollars tick. In Silicon Valley, dopamine is laced into everything where—like Kim—it enjoys cult status. Perhaps the best example of this is the iGen favourite: Snapstreaks. Snapchat, which has over 240 million active users, has embedded Snapstreaks, a feature that measures how many consecutive days you and your friend send Snaps to one another. The longer you go without breaking the streak, the more Snapchat rewards you. 'My friends get really annoyed if we break a streak,' says Bani, 'so the first thing I do when I wake up in the morning is send a message to all my streaks.' Since no one wants to

---

[*] Incidentally, the tagline is somewhat scientifically accurate. A glass of Pepsi contains roughly nine teaspoons of sugar resulting in huge bursts of dopamine that make you crave the drink more.

break a long streak, the more time you invest in creating a streak, the more you need to keep going—the perfect recipe for endless Snapchat usage. It's happening all over the world. Our children are consuming bottomless bowls of tech junk laced with so much dopamine that they just can't stop eating it. Incidentally, this is not some classified fact unknown to the folks at Snapchat; Evan Spiegel, the Snapchat CEO, allows his own children just ninety minutes of screen time per week[3] even as Snapchat hungrily gobbles up the time of millions of young people globally. So perhaps the next time your kid insists that 'everyone is doing it', you can assure them that the Snapchat CEO's kids are not! But it's not just Snapchat, almost every app is finetuned to maximize addiction. And yet, these apps are so ubiquitous that banning your teen from using them will likely isolate your kid. You might as well make them live under a rock.

But back to app product design. In this design, nothing is off limits. After a protracted battle with insomnia, my friend Dipti confesses that her late-night Netflix addiction is beginning to impact her job performance. Our brains don't discriminate between different kinds of pleasure, and once again, it's dopamine that is released when we binge-watch *Succession* or *Bridgerton*. 'You experience a pseudo-addiction to the show because you develop cravings for dopamine,' says[4] psychologist Dr Renee Carr. Dipti's cravings get so bad that she has her spouse hide the TV remote every night. But for Wilmot Reed Hastings Jr, Netflix's co-founder and executive chairman, Dipti's insomnia is proof that his product design is working. Recently, Hastings suggested that Netflix's most formidable competitor is the human need for sleep: 'We are really competing with sleep on the margin,'[5] he said. Reading that sentence from Hastings made me do a double take. Nothing is sacred anymore—not even our sleep.

The 'Magic of Maybe'

In some sense, hacking our dopamine pathways is an old trick; casino owners have exploited it for decades. So have drug dealers, ask any cocaine addict about the dopamine rush. But Big Tech and casinos have yet another bio-hacking technique in common: they both use 'variable reward systems' to keep their customers craving for more. This sounds complicated but stay with me, the premise is simple. It works like this: since you don't know exactly *when* you will win at the slot machine (or get a like on your Insta post), your brain is incentivized to keep checking. That's it, that's the whole game and it works! Think about how you feel right after you post something on Instagram. You're waiting for validation through likes and comments, but you don't know when those might appear. Maybe there will be likes, maybe not. It's also part of why you reach for your cellphone constantly—maybe you'll be rewarded by a message, maybe not. Robert Sapolsky, neuroendocrinology researcher and professor at Stanford University, calls it the 'magic of maybe'. 'Dopamine,' he says, 'is not about pleasure, it's about the *anticipation* of pleasure.' The magic of maybe is exactly why I kept refreshing and checking my Christmas post during the ride to dinner. Maybe I would get some likes, maybe I wouldn't, and so I just *had* to check.

Unlike unintelligent slot machines, the AI embedded in social media apps puts the variable rewards system on steroids. For example, Instagram often withholds likes on your photos so that it can deliver them to your inbox in big bunches. Think of it like this: you post a photo of your dinner at the fancy new sushi restaurant. You're eager to see a response and keep returning to Insta to check for likes. Instagram recognizes this behaviour and withholds the responses, essentially priming your pathways for a big dopamine rush when after a few empty checks, you finally see a big bunch of likes. It's the digital equivalent of feeling sad that all your friends forgot your birthday and then walking into a big surprise party—your initial disappointment makes the surprise all the better! Instagram (and many other platforms) know this and therefore, deliver the most dopamine-laden experience just when you've been feeling ignored. 'These unnaturally large rewards are not filtered in the brain—they go directly into the brain and overstimulate, which can generate addiction,' explains Cambridge University professor Wolfram Schultz. 'When that happens, we lose our willpower. Evolution has not prepared our brains for these drugs, so they become overwhelmed and screwed up. We are abusing a useful and necessary system. We shouldn't do it, even though we can.'[6]

While the tricks aren't new (casinos have been around for a while), this is the first time in human history that we're handing over slot machines to kids. There is more dopamine circulating in the teen brain than at any other stage in life and this is also the exact time that most parents give their children a smartphone. It's the perfect storm. We have taken something so maddeningly habit-forming, so infuriatingly addictive, powered by the most powerful AI on the planet and placed it in the palms of children everywhere. We typically do this when they're twelve or thirteen years old, well before their brains are mature enough to develop any natural defences. And then we give them a charger to make sure the dope never runs out.

Data: The New Gold Mine

But what's the point of all this? Why does Big Tech care about keeping us up at night, jacked up on dopamine and addicted to our phones? Well, nothing in life is ever free and tech companies didn't become the most profitable companies in human history by accident. The growth of many tech companies—all of social media, for instance—is directly dependent on collecting our data in order to sell us things from eczema creams to beachside villas in Goa. The platforms on which our children are spending so much time, forging identities and looking for validation are all owned by major corporations. While we are busy editing our Insta photos, these companies are busy selling us products and in a very real sense, shaping our value systems. They have a deeply vested interest in us sharing as much information as possible so that they can, in turn, sell us more products that are personalized to the information that we have shared. You will never pay to create a social media account because Big Tech doesn't need your pennies. Not when you're giving them the most powerful currency in the world: your data. You have likely spent today using your phone as a communication device, an information service, a broadcasting platform and even a personal secretary. Virtually every time you have used your phone, you have leaked data. You may as well be leaking pure gold.

Leaking personal data is now just the cost of being connected to the Internet, and cumulatively you have leaked so much data that Big Tech knows everything about you.* Your medical history, your taste in jokes, who you love, what you fear and everything in between. It's all part of the expanding file that Big Tech has on you. Based on the newspaper articles you read, the algorithm knows who you will vote for as PM. How many microseconds you spend on an Instastory tells it what you find sexy. Almost certainly, Big Tech knows you better than your mother.** Every app that you use, from NDTV and CricBuzz to WhatsApp, is competing for the same prize—your data. And as your data can be directly monetized into advertising revenue, the race for your attention is only getting more competitive. Targeted advertising—using your data to sell you more products—has helped turn Facebook and others into the most profitable companies on Earth. This, even though none of us have ever paid one rupee for our social media accounts.

Of course, one could take the view that none of this is coercion; after all, we agree to the 'terms and conditions' when signing up for an account. But these agreements are purposefully obtuse, deliberately designed to be so dense

---

* Turning off Microphone access (Settings → Privacy and Security → Microphone) will help protect your privacy especially when you use social media.
** This is a reminder to use your phone for good and call your mother.

that nobody really bothers reading them. As a result, we mindlessly click 'I agree' in the end, and from then on, Big Tech largely owns our opinions, photographs, locations and everything else in perpetuity. Our data is now theirs—we've given them the keys to the gold mine.

On a WhatsApp call, I'm complaining to my gym trainer that my Punjabi heritage has gifted me with stubborn belly fat that won't budge no matter how much time I spend on the treadmill. An hour later, I open YouTube to find an advertisement for a laser liposuction company. 'Free Consult!' it yells in a large red font, 'Remove that belly fat!' Later, I send a message to the paediatrician about my son's rash, and the next time I open Facebook, my feed is filled with advertisements for eczema rash creams. Every app I use is listening, understanding me better and creating a personalized, 'stickier' experience. The Internet lives in us as much as we live on the Internet, and in the future, me trying liposuction may not be my decision. The 2020 US presidential election was a testimony to the fact that many people supported candidates that their social media feeds chose for them. Essentially, the phone made the decision.

Speaking of the US, the leadership team of my alma mater reveals that a double major in computer science and psychology is currently all the rage in elite US colleges. Computer science with psychology? I'm surprised! During my college days, I remember the nerdy IT folks practically living on a different planet from the artsy psych majors. But today, top universities from Yale to Penn are combining disciplines to create that most formidable human: a coder who understands the human psyche. Not only do they know how to code, but *they*

know how you think. These are the same folks—designers, engineers and product managers working on your apps.*
Tristan Harris, a former Google employee now widely known as 'Silicon Valley's conscience', puts it bluntly when he says, 'a handful of people working at a handful of tech companies steer the thoughts of billions of people every day'.[7] Tristan's warnings are echoed by Geoffrey Hinton, another former Google employee. Hinton is regarded as the 'godfather of AI' and he recently quit his job at Google because he was alarmed by the emerging dangers of AI. '[I] can now just speak freely about what the dangers might be,' said Hinton.[8]

While we should take individual responsibility for controlling our phone usage, it's not so easy. There are literally battalions of people on the other side of the screen—armed with deep pockets, access to our data, pathbreaking AI and intimate knowledge of human neurocircuitry—who are entirely focused on breaking our self-control. As Israeli historian and author of *Sapiens*, Yuval Noah Harari, states: 'the smartest people in the world, over the last few years [have been] working on the problem of how to hack your brain and grab your attention. And they have been successful [as] the smartphone is really the gate, the window to your mind.'[9] As things stand, we've all thrown the windows open to the raging storm.

---

* Many Silicon Valley luminaries, including top executives at Instagram, Facebook and Google took 'persuasive technology' classes at Stanford. This included studying clicker training for dogs in which clicks are associated with rewards. Yes, it's all clicking into place now!

Only Beauty, No Beast:
The Frenzy of Filters

My friend Natasha is a legit fashionista. When we last met, she was casually dressed in a high street dress and boots, the whole outfit pulled together with tortoiseshell sunglass from a small boutique in Paris and a bohochic bag handmade in Udaipur. If I wore the same outfit, I'd look homeless. Natasha looked lit, so when she announced her Instagram fashion account, I lit up. Perhaps, I could finally learn how to achieve a non-homeless look. Within a few days, the account was running, and I headed over to Natasha's first post, where she was showcasing the season's hottest leather skirt. But something was off. In fact, something was jarring. The problem wasn't the top. Or the skirt. It certainly wasn't those ridiculously cute boots. I cocked my head and looked again. What was it? And then I saw it. It was Natasha's legs. The faintest hint of cellulite was visible on her thighs, along with tiny bumps on her knees. What was wrong with me? Was I startled because her legs looked . . . natural?

Tuning into FaceTune

'I don't want to look natural. Nothing about my life is natural . . . I *need* to be looking extra.' I have moved on from Natasha's legs and am now watching Maral, a massively popular influencer. She's conducting a YouTube tutorial on how to look 'extra' in every photo. Essentially how to achieve InstaFace.

Virtually every woman with an Internet connection knows InstaFace. It's there, smiling sexily in your subconscious as you unzip your makeup bag and examine your face, the ultimate blank canvas. Cheekbones: contoured. Nose: slimmed. Lips: plumped and winged eyeliner flicked just so. You keep going until InstaFace smiles back at you from the mirror and your face seems optional. The reflection looks like a poreless Cleopatra crossbred with a sexy kitten. *Purrfect*. And if you want to know just how popular the trend is, here's a quick fact: #instaface has over 1.2 million posts. That's several hundred thousand posts more than #gandhi. Predictably, InstaFace started at that inexhaustible font of all Internet trends: the Kardashians. Soon, every makeup brand was tripping over their bronzers to promote it. The Internet exploded with tutorials on how highlighters and blush sticks could make your life look like one jaunty sun-dipped ride with no pores.

But make-up is so basic now. In fact, Maral doesn't even use any make-up in her YouTube tutorials; she, and millions of others have found a much easier way to sex up their photos. Enter FaceTune. 'Normally, I zoom into my face first and see what I want to do with my . . . face,' says Maral. Her hands move at lightning speed, slimming her nose, tilting her eyes and plumping her lips in seconds. She's zooming, pinching and snatching like a pro. 'My cheeks are super swollen and puffy,' laments Maral. FaceTune comes to the rescue like a benevolent fairy godmother; a few quick swipes and her problems are solved. Tap, tap, tap. Puffiness gone.

My problems begin when Maral starts talking about her drooping nose. 'I hate that little droop,' she says, 'I hate that s**t.' My fingers reach to check my nose for a droop.

Do noses droop?

Does *my* nose droop?

I feel like my nose droops.

And bam! Just like that, I've been *influenced*.

British YouTuber Em Ford's viral video challenge 'Redefine Pretty' asked several young women to participate in a fascinating experiment. The participating women had their brains scanned while being shown flawless, airbrushed photos of models—exactly the sort of photos that we see on Insta every day. Researchers wanted to understand what happens to women's brains when they look at these photos. What they discovered was staggering: as the women looked at these filtered photos, *MRI scans suggested that they were experiencing trauma*. The findings were consistent; even though the women *knew* they were looking at airbrushed photos, the bottom line was clear—they were being traumatized. The findings are startling, especially for iGen girls whose Instagram feeds are brimming with edited photos. Without realizing it, *they are being traumatized every day.*

In the dinosaur days, it was the sole prerogative of movie stars to make us feel insecure about ourselves.

Today, even the neighbour's Instagram posts can traumatize iGen. After all, this is a generation for whom digital perception is key; Google reports that every third photo taken by iGen is a selfie. Driven by selfie culture, plastic surgeons have seen massive increases in patients under thirty, with this being celebrated as the heyday of plastic surgery.[10] And even though we were locked up at home, the pandemic seems to have made us more aware of how we look. Staring at my reflection during those video calls, I watched my face on the screen: how I moved, how I talked and how my mouth seemed crooked as the family sang one more round of *happy birthday* during those endless Zoom birthday calls. Which of us didn't notice our odd teeth or emerging wrinkles—details that we might have missed before? But pandemic or not, iGen has always cared *deeply* about how their faces look on a screen; after all, that's where they hang out most.

As more women contour their way to #instaface, the chasm between Instagram and reality widens. And with this widening gap comes yet another parenting challenge. You and I know that chasing perfection is a fool's errand with only one sureshot outcome: lifelong disappointment. But who's going to tell the kids especially when the illusion of perfection is so readily available? I'm on the phone with Sania, a fifteen-year-old self-confessed 'FaceTune queen' from Mumbai. She tells me she uses FaceTune because she wants to look 'just flawless'. I ask whether she manages to look flawless in real life too. 'It's much harder to be flawless IRL,' she admits, 'that's why I prefer to just stay home and talk to my friends on Insta.' I see her point. It's difficult to live life looking flawless but morphing your face on a screen is so easy! And free! And rewarding! You get so many likes that you feel like you are the centre of the digital universe. Remember the dopamine hits we discussed earlier? Sania doesn't know it, but every time she gets a like, her brain releases dopamine giving her that giddy, feel-good feeling. Soon enough, she'll crave another hit and head back to FaceTune to morph another picture. Then she'll wait around for the likes to pile up again. No wonder we're all hanging around Instagram like meth addicts.

Talking to Sania about looking flawless reminds me of how uncomfortable I felt when I saw Natasha's non-airbrushed legs: filters that smooth every pore are making the texture of human skin intolerable. Will future generations see only picture-perfect cyborgs who live nothing but their jaunty #sunkissed #bestlife every day? If we make only one version of beauty acceptable, then by definition, will everything else be considered ugly? Is perfection simply the elimination of every imperfection?

Maral's video tutorial continues as I think about these questions. She is now fixing the hairline on her photo. 'Look at how big my forehead looks!' she exclaims. And before I can wearily lift my hand to measure my own forehead, she has reshaped hers. With her face satisfactorily tuned, Maral now starts to tune her body. The first thing to get tuned is her butt since she hasn't done her BBL (Brazilian Butt Lift) yet. 'I'm going to get a Brazilian butt lift anyway, so, honestly, this is what I'll look like in a few months,' she says. Clearly, some convoluted butt ethics are at play. Maral quickly adjusts her breasts, snatches her waist à la Kim, and slims her arms. She is now the embodiment of #slimthicc, an Internet beauty standard that expects women to have a waist the size of their wrist with boobs the size of the Titanic's hull!

I won't lie: Maral looks incredible. She just doesn't look human.

Ana and Mia

I talk to Arushi, a seventeen-year-old from Bengaluru who has been struggling with anorexia for years. 'Three years ago, I pledged allegiance to Ana,' she says, explaining how it all began. I know what she's talking about; I've spent weeks researching Ana (anorexia) and Mia (bulimia). In the digital age, online forums have given anthropomorphic names to these eating disorders. Ana and Mia are practically goddesses in these online groups, such is the devotion they command. 'Anorexia is a religion here,' explains Arushi about her online forum. Ana and Mia are their saviours, the messiahs who will help these young girls feel whole again. That's why Arushi and others need to pledge allegiance at Ana and Mia's altars.' I ask Arushi if she remembers her pledge. 'Of course. I used to say it aloud every day. I posted it online too, but my mom made me delete the posts. Do you want me to say it?' And before I can stop her from repeating it, Arushi says, 'I pledge allegiance to Ana. I SHALL NOT, I SHALL NOT want food. Ana will perfect me.'

Listening to Arushi is like being in a time warp. I feel sucked into a wormhole, zapped back to my fourteen-year-old self when I fantasized about having a concave belly and protruding ribs. All I wanted was to be a little thinner, a little bonier. I remember running my fingers over my hipbones, softly tracing their protrusion to see if they could push out just a little more. It was thrilling to lift my shirt to count my ribs, and I rejoiced when my clavicle pushed through my skin in sharp angles. It became easy to repeat 'I'm full' ad nauseum when my parents pleaded with me to eat. 'The last thing you ate was two days ago,' said my mother, herself nauseated with worry. Words like anorexia weren't written into our dictionaries then or perhaps they were in books that my family didn't have on their shelves. The disease remained invisible, and soon, I started disappearing too.

A few months later, I gave up food. Or rather, I gave up any food that was not directly linked to my survival. We still didn't use words like anorexia. My new normal became water and an apple over two days. Every morning, I lifted my shirt to count my ribs, and that number became the sum total of my achievements. My parents put together the usual buffet of strategies—grilling me, serving up a dizzying variety of food and soon enough, the doctors and tonics followed.

Through it all, my parents' dinner parties continued but I had stopped going into the kitchen. By now, the smell of food was revolting. I would sit in the dining room, touching the fancy napkins, the ones that only made it out of the drawer for guests. The napkins were white with lace corners, starched solid from years of whitening powder. Something once soft had now become stiff and brittle. One of the napkins had a rusty spot— probably from Mom's famous mutton curry—and when no one was looking, I threw it away. The thought of curry made me feel sick.

'Why won't you eat?' was the question *du jour* that showed up unfailingly on the menu every day. I was quiet. How could I explain to my parents that I wasn't being stubborn? I had ingested too much of what pretty teenage girls look like, and now I was too full. It's not that I *wouldn't* eat. I simply *couldn't* eat.

While my condition improved, it took time. I had learned how to become my own worst critic. The body dysmorphia, in particular, persisted even after I resumed eating. For years, I would walk into clothing stores and head straight to the larger sizes. 'No, no. That's not your size. You're an S or even XS,' the sales assistant would say delightedly, as though she were awarding me the gold medal. I would shake my head because when I looked at my reflection, it was like looking in a funhouse mirror— I saw something totally different.

Working through my body image issues has taken time and practice. Learning to eat again has meant rehabilitating both my body and mind. I stopped buying weighing scales. I learned to celebrate my body, with its squishy flanks and skinny ankles, for what it is—mine. But even decades later, some days are harder than others. When my friend Puja looks at a photo of me with another friend, she says, 'You're looking great, Neha! You look even thinner than her.' In that moment, I have to exhale and continue to unlearn the two subliminal messages that I have internalized over the years: 1) Thin is good, and 2) This is a competition. I shake off the image of skinny gladiators wrestling each other in a pit and head to the kitchen to fix myself a snack.

Experiencing anorexia in the 1990s is proof enough that Instagram and FaceTune didn't invent eating disorders. But while toxic beauty standards predate the Internet, social media is indisputably promoting them at unprecedented rates.[11] Something happened around 2010 that made depression and suicide rates among teen girls skyrocket.[12] Consider the evidence: between 2009 and 2012, Facebook added the like button, Twitter added its retweet button and, perhaps most damningly, 2012 was the year that Instagram was released on Android, mopping up a million downloads in twenty-four hours! While correlation is not causation, experts who have spent years researching teen health observe that the timing of this shocking crash in mental health for teenage girls can only point to the stratospheric rise of social media. Arushi says it was the hashtag #thinspo on Instagram that ignited things for her. 'I would follow thinspiration accounts for days, obsessed with their bodies and lives. I just wanted to be like them.' I know what she means— I've counted my ribs too. But luckily for me, I didn't have an endless 'Explore' page crammed with photos and videos, fuelled by an algorithm insistent on sending me down a bottomless pit of radioactive content.

It takes me several attempts but Arushi eventually lets me into one of her Ana forums. Most of these forums are closely guarded and access is restricted to those who have pledged allegiance. It is here that many of the Anas and Mias teach one another how to starve. I log in and scroll through the Anas discussing the weight of water and what kind of surface is best for placing weighing scales. The Mias share advice on timing your vomit: too soon after eating and nothing comes up, but waiting too long means you've digested too much.

There is much to learn, and there's a teacher behind every keyboard. I can only spend a few minutes in there before I start to feel triggered.

'Nothing tastes as good as skinny feels,' says one poster.

'Hungry to bed. Hungry to rise. Makes a girl a smaller size.'

'Empty stomachs weigh less.'

'Go to bed without dinner, wake up thinner.'

'I'm going to try and stay under 300 calories today. Who wants to starve with me?'

And then I see the Ana who is fasting for likes and comments: 'One like = one hour of fasting. One reply = two hours,' she says. I log off.

Eating disorders are some of the most private afflictions human beings experience. The feeling of being caged in your body is hard to explain, and you instinctively know, deep in your brittle bones, that most people won't know how to deal with it. They won't be able to swallow it, and if they do, they'll find it hard to digest. There was a sense of isolation associated with eating disorders in the 1990s, but now these forums come together to celebrate them. Isolation or celebration—I don't know which one is more damaging.

Insta Sexy

Since 2019, Instagram, owned by Meta (formerly Facebook, Inc.) has been studying how the platform affects the mental health of its youngest users, especially teenage girls. The results are deeply damaging. Internal documents accessed by top journalists reveal[13] that Insta understands the toxicity of its product. 'We make body image issues worse for one in three teen girls,' reads the headline of one internal slide. '32 per cent of teen girls said that when they felt bad about their bodies, Instagram made them feel worse,' says another internal memo. Instagram's internal research reveals that the 'tendency to share only the best moments, a pressure to look perfect and an addictive product can send teens spiralling toward eating disorders, an unhealthy sense of their bodies and depression'. *This is the company's research on itself.* Let that sink in for a moment. Although these memos have been leaked and published by leading newspapers, Meta continues to downplay the results and refuses to make its research on Instagram public. But the jury is out, and independent research confirms that Instagram is the worst social media network for mental health and well-being.[14] And 28 per cent of iGen in India are accessing Instagram more than ten times a day.[15]

As every parent knows, social media's bad bits are often bundled with the good, making it that classic double-edged sword that is impossible to discard and dangerous to embrace. A fourteen-year-old recently killed herself after watching videos and images of suicide, self-harm and depressive content online for months.[16] 'This is Instagram literally giving Molly ideas,' said the family's lawyer who squarely blames Meta for the teenager's death. And while Molly killed herself on the other side of the world, Aadhya in Chennai told me that she started cutting herself at the age of eleven after watching videos that glamorize depression for the young. I know this is frightening stuff for any parent; I feel it too. Through most of my conversation with Aadhya, I had to keep calm by forcing myself to slowly exhale repeatedly. Jean Twenge, researcher and author has been studying the effects of social media for years. She's trying to figure out why ER visits for self-harm like cutting have tripled for girls between the ages of ten and fourteen. 'There's kind of two different schools of thought on this. That it's the specific things that teens are doing on their phones that are the problem. Or it could be just the sheer amount of time that they're spending on their phones that is the problem,' she says. Of course, social media isn't the only reason that kids are drowning in this mental health tsunami, but it's definitely fanning the waves. To what extent? The jury is still out.

Not that we need juries to tell us what we already know. You feel like a loser if you are not winning at something, twinning with someone or just generally having an #EPIC moment. Our Insta stories brim over with gorgeous celebrities, stunning beaches and hashtagged moments that often make us despair the reality of our own ordinary, badly lit lives. Several times an hour, in the car or at home while lying on the couch, we compare our dullest moments to filtered photos from friends and contrived content from celebrities. Everyone seems to be having their moment and watching these highlight reels has left us all craving short-term popularity, no matter the cost. And so, we keep trying to be somebody on social media, but there is always somebody who is more 'somebody' than us. It's impossible to win, but it seems even more impossible not to try.

I'm still thinking about the mental diet that we are feeding our young girls when I come across a recent study that reveals that 80 per cent of ten-year-old girls in America have dieted at some point.[17] *Eighty per cent of ten year olds*—that statistic stops me in my tracks. I decided to conduct some independent, unscientific research with a few girls between the ages of eight and eleven. My question to them is simple: what do you like most about your body? An easy question that should get some easy answers. The eight year olds are quick to answer. 'I like my legs because I won the medal on sports day,' is the first response. The ten year olds respond differently. They hang out together in little groups and take their time. 'Are you asking what we like or what we *don't* like?' asks one of them, suspicious of my intent. 'I want to know what you like. Tell me what *you like,*' I insist. The answers come in wobbly and shaky. 'I like my teeth, but I don't like anything else,' someone finally says. She has just turned eleven. What happens to girls in just a couple of years? What messages do they learn so quickly?

Zoya's piano teacher has sent her some YouTube practice videos to watch before her lesson. I'm with her in the room as she clicks on the link and waits for the advertisement to end before the piano tutorial can begin. 'The secret to losing weight . . .' smiles the impossibly cheerful young woman in the YouTube ad, '. . . is simply to eat less!' I realize then that YouTube's algorithms have probably profiled Zoya as a young girl and served up this content. 'That's it! Just eat less . . .' continues the advertisement but luckily, she clicks on 'Skip Ad' before the product can flash on the screen. The room suddenly fills with the sound of a piano melody, and I ask Zoya what she thinks the product might have been.

'Maybe a diet juice or a diet pill,' she replies. Clearly, she's seen this stuff before. She looks hesitant, and I sense that she wants to say more. 'I know that stuff isn't good for you, but the lady just looked so happy.' I look at my tween and realize that she's right. In advertisements across the world, we make starvation look cheerful. 'Lose weight, feel great' is the subliminal tagline of every diet product. And millions of our girls start to think that weight is inversely proportional to happiness.

Recently, I was on a celebratory trip with a few of my girlfriends. Our little group had many reasons to make merry: one of us was getting married and another had recently been promoted to COO of her company. With dinner done, we decided to change into something comfortable before reconvening. Everyone was sharing rooms except for one who had insisted that she needed a room to herself. Changed and eager to regroup, I went to collect her. As soon as I knocked on the door, I heard it: the sound of dinner being heaved up, over and over again. Suddenly it all made sense: the constant mints, the frequent flushing and the insistence on a separate room. I continued to knock, and after several long minutes, she finally responded. We looked at each other silently through the crack of that barely opened door, a former Ana and a current Mia. Then we went back to celebrating each other's achievements, never once bringing up what was eating us from within.

I Like Me When You Like Me

How would you react if I told you there was a big prize up for grabs for completing a simple task? 'It'll only take a few seconds,' I'd say. You might be interested until I told you what the task was: you had slowly and thoroughly lick an airport toilet seat. 'Full disclaimer,' I would continue, as you shuddered in disgust, 'the "big prize" isn't money or a mansion or even a shiny new car. It's a few hearts on Instagram and five minutes of online fame.' I can see you pick up your phone and delete my number. But even as you walk away from me, you should know that young people across the world have filmed themselves licking airplane toilet seats and running their tongues on metro handlebars. It was called the Coronavirus challenge and like the pandemic, it went viral. Not as breathtakingly grotesque but just as dangerous was the Blackout challenge which dared TikTokers to hold their breath until they fainted (a ten year old died). Then there was the Fire Mirror challenge which required spraying flammable liquid on a mirror and setting it on fire (several tweens suffered third-degree burns). And who can forget the Rotating Corn challenge where participants ate corn from the edge of a rotating drill (one person accidentally drilled out his front teeth while another ripped the hair from her scalp). A group of teenagers I spoke to had taken the Cinnamon challenge (eating a tablespoon of cinnamon without drinking anything). 'I nearly died,' said one of the boys with a laugh. I asked if they would consider hanging out of a building window for a challenge. 'Yeah, it'll make a cool pic,' was the nonchalant reply.

Growing up, which one of us wasn't asked, 'SO! If your friend jumped into a well, would you jump too?' It was a rhetorical question, perfected by every Indian parent and exquisitely designed to induce an immediate apology with a head hung in shame. But today, if jumping into a well meant earning likes, well, there might be a line at the well. Caught as they are between childhood and adulthood, teenagers are particularly sensitive to their social environment. And so, suspended between life stages, clutching their new phones and shaky ideas of self-worth, iGen are often sitting ducks desperate for online validation. For many teenagers across the world, those little hearts matter enough to jump into wells, lick airport toilets and set themselves on fire. Mystified by these challenges, a news reporter asked the TikTok influencer behind the Coronavirus toilet seat challenge why she started something so absurd. 'I was tired of that b**ch Corona getting more publicity than me. I'm the real celebrity,'[18] she replied.

Everyone on the Insta Red Carpet

Remember when Facebook was launched? It was a revolutionary idea to create a social *network* where you could connect with existing friends, reconnect with lost ones and maybe even make a few new buddies. All of us did all of those things. I recall using Facebook to chat with the old school gang, reconnect with my college roommate who was volunteering in Africa and get life updates from an ex-boyfriend. But everything changed when the iPhone and Instagram launched in quick succession. Platforms went from being *social networks* to *social media* where instead of connecting with those in your circle, you became a media product to be created and consumed often by those outside of your network. Ian Bogost from *Atlantic* urges us to think of the change like this: in the social networking era, connections were essential, driving both content creation and consumption. But the social-media era seeks the thinnest, most soluble connections possible, just enough to allow the content to flow.[19] Essentially, we've all become mini media companies packaging ourselves for the consumption of strangers who land on our pages on the whims of an anonymous algorithm.

In this age, where everything is a brand, social media has turned everyone into a (potential) celebrity. If there is no one to take photos of us, we take selfies and become our overeager paparazzi as we walk ourselves down the Insta red carpet. I'm speaking to Gulshan, twenty-eight, who has a significant social media following. She posts about lifestyle and fashion but mostly she's semi-famous for being semi-famous. In her latest post, she's in the sun-kissed Maldives with tousled beach hair and movie-star sunglasses. A Rihanna quote about loving your body is the caption. 'Likes are life, babe!' she laughs when I ask if she cares about the reactions to her posts. I've spent some time on Gulshan's account, so I ask her about a couple of commenters who always make an appearance in the comment section with sugary comments about her. Enough sugar to give anyone diabetes. There's something sycophantically oily, almost unctuous about these commenters and they are invariably the first to appear after she posts. 'Yeah, those are paid comments. When people see nice comments, they also feel like saying something nice.' I turn the thought over in my mind like a coin. In the past, I have had friends ask me to comment on their posts as a way to kickstart the comment section, but this is the first time a friend has acknowledged paying a professional for the service. I ask Gulshan if she considers this fake. 'What "fake"?' she replies dismissively, 'We all spend two hours a day taking photos, then applying every filter possible to get more likes. Isn't that also fake?' Good point.

Speaking of fake, buying followers is supremely easy—it isn't some dark-web deal done with cloaks and daggers. A simple Google search yields dozens of providers who offer cheap services with many of them offering 5000 Insta followers for approximately Rs 2000, backed with instant delivery and a money-back guarantee. Even ordering onions online doesn't give you that. If you want to add faces to your followers, head over to Generated.Photos or ThisPersonDoesNotExist.com. There, for the price of a cup of coffee, you can buy the face you need and adjust it to your preference.

Young or old, hot or not, brown or with a frown. Companies like Rosebud AI can animate these faces and make them do whatever you like. As the *New York Times* reports, 'Given the pace of improvement, it's easy to imagine a not-so-distant future in which we are confronted with not just single portraits of fake people but whole collections of them—at a party with fake friends, hanging out with their fake dogs, holding their fake babies. It will become increasingly difficult to tell who is real online and who is a figment of a computer's imagination.'

Things are so murky in this department that even Elon Musk is struggling. When buying out Twitter, Elon insisted that one of his top priorities would be to weed out the millions of 'spam bots' or fake accounts that are crawling all over the platform. One problem with that plan: it would cut Musk's own following nearly to half![20] The fakes are everywhere, and just like the Gucci handbags that sell in basement markets, it's really hard to tell them from the originals. Head over to your friend's account, the one who somehow has several thousand followers. You'll never know if those followers are real or simply thousands of bots bought for the price of lunch to feed a sense of fake celebrityhood.

All the World Is a Stage

But what comes of this obsession with our own perceived celebrityhood? The Greek myth of Narcissus tells us about a handsome young man who became dangerously obsessed with his reflection. After glimpsing his image in a pool of water, Narcissus becomes so enamoured by his beauty that he can't bear to look away. He preens and pines, ultimately dying of starvation and leaving us with a dire warning in the word 'narcissist'. The analogy is obvious. Replace the pool with Instagram and there we are: Narcissus, by the millions. Narcissus in that we are endlessly staring at our screens, enamoured with the idea of our celebrityhood, pining away until our brains atrophy. Researchers estimate that 80 per cent of social media is self-focused[21]—*my* car, *my* vacation, *my* opinion, *my* friends, *my* champagne brunch. As anyone who has posted an Instagram story knows, much of this is performative. We post about ourselves constantly but are more disconnected from ourselves than ever before. We have, quite literally, lost ourselves in the performance.

This disconnectedness has consequences, especially for iGen. Until a few decades ago, the biggest threats facing teenagers were drunk driving, teen pregnancies and smoking. The rates for all of these have fallen dramatically and replaced by a single problem: mental health disorders. Jean Twenge, psychologist and professor, puts it bluntly: 'iGen [is] on the brink of the worst mental-health crisis in decades. Much of this deterioration can be traced to their phones.'[22] But what is it about our phones that is creating this tsunami of mental health crises?

Disconnected with Ourselves

Fifteen-year-old Rohan recollects the time when he was at his family's Diwali party having a great time. The family had gathered for the first time since the pandemic; his grandmother had cooked everyone's favourite food, the music was loud, and the love was strong. And that's when he saw the post. 'I just happened to scroll Insta and saw it. A bunch of my friends were at a party to which I wasn't invited. And boom! My night was ruined.

I went into a room and just kept looking at my phone. My family tried asking me what was wrong, and I didn't know what to tell them—it was so stupid,' he says. Abruptly disconnected from the family gathering, he says he spent the rest of the night tracking his friends to figure out exactly who was at the party. Rohan is a self-aware teenager with a timer that limits his Instagram use. 'All Insta does is suck my time away and give me FOMO,' he points out. But even though Rohan finds Insta toxic, he can't give up the app. 'All the news is on Insta before it's updated anywhere else. Not being on Insta means being totally cut off,' he says. I know what he means. Social media is the ultimate mixed blessing: disconnecting even as it connects us.

I recently attended a restaurant launch in Mumbai, entering alongside three fashionably dressed young women, none of whom seemed interested in introductions as they swished past. 'Ananya we'll use your phone, babe,' cooed one of them. And so, I met Ananya. It was a chic eatery in the ever-evolving Worli, and I was looking forward to sampling the restaurant's much-touted bao. Before we could greet our hosts, the young women— ably led by Ananya—immediately occupied themselves with sussing out the most Instagrammable spot in the restaurant. I watched as they took what seemed like dozens of selfies and then sashayed out. No bye, no bao, but most likely a fantastic Instagram story. I was reminded of psychologist Dr Saliha Afridi's words about social media, 'These days, it's not know yourself, it's show yourself!'*

---

* And similarly, it's not enough to wish someone on their birthday, you have to be seen SHOWING that affection. Recently, Deepika Padukone received backlash when she skipped posting for her

she said. But the trouble with *showing* a moment instead of *knowing* a moment is that it minimizes the time and awareness for introspection. As content creator Rohan Joshi says, 'It sucks to interrogate every moment you experience through the lens of "would this make a good post?" Or joke? Or reel? Or any form of dopamine nugget at all? Manufacturing dopamine nuggets is a dangerous business. First, you get people hooked on your specific flavour of dopamine. Then, more dangerously, you start to get high on your own supply.'[23]

The same week, I am in the mall, shopping for clothes with Zoya. I cast a glance over at a stack of t-shirts; 'ICON' screams the white shirt, the words foiled in gold. 'VIP' yells the green crop top. Popular culture increasingly exhorts us—and our children—to be (fake) famous by posting on social media as though we were brands, icons and even VIPs. We spend hours every day trying to be noticed in social media's crowded marketplace, performing stunts for the approval of strangers and buying blue ticks for the approval of our egos. All of us—children included—are being encouraged to seek the opinions of people who don't know us. And so, we wait for the likes to add up so we can figure out how much to like ourselves.

Self-obsession and paradoxical self-disconnection don't bode well for tweens and teens, as they are caught in a life stage in which they are testing boundaries and experimenting with new identities. At a time when their own identity is a work in progress, social media offers

---

husband Ranveer's birthday. 'Marital problems?' whispered the Internet when she didn't publicly show what is likely a very private wish.

them the option to be someone else: a lifestyle influencer, a fashionista, a travel connoisseur . . . the options are endless. In a recent survey, 64 per cent of tweens and teens in India admitted to reinventing themselves online by trying to appear older, or creating a fake profile or posting photos that are not their own.[24] Many of the teens I interviewed spoke about cultivating their 'personal brand' suggesting that *who they are often depends on what sells best*. While this provides some interesting career opportunities (which we'll discuss in a later chapter), it will often be the comment section that shapes iGen's identity before they've had time to shape themselves. Before they can do the hard work of forming their own identities, our kids have to contend with the perceptions and opinions of strangers from around the globe. That's overwhelming on a good day.

Disconnected from Others

Human beings thrive best with approximately 150 social connections. But, social media gives us access to potentially two billion social connections at any time! This constant feedback pings our neural circuits in a way that the human mind simply isn't built to handle. People just aren't meant to talk to one another this much, writes Ian Bogost. 'From being asked to review every product you buy to believing that every tweet or Instagram image warrants likes, comments or follows, social media [has] produced a positively unhinged, sociopathic rendition of human sociality. That's no surprise, I guess, given that the model was forged in the fires of Big Tech companies such as Facebook, where sociopathy is a design philosophy.'

Many of the 'connections' that social media forges aren't real connections at all but brittle, one-way roads that lead straight to loneliness. I walk that road too. When Ali announced on her birthday that she was expecting twins, my first reaction was delight mixed with indignation. 'Why didn't you tell me sooner?' I thought, somewhat upset. Through the next few months, I was with Ali through her pregnancy journey, going along as she went to her prenatal appointments and readied the twins' nursery. I made sure to check in on her especially when she was expecting results from a big scan or test. Of course, I was ecstatic when Ali's babies were born, healthy and full-term, with the most beautiful names— Rio and Sol. Here's the thing though: Ali Maffucci is not my friend; in fact, we've never even met. Ali is a food influencer on Instagram, and I am one of her many thousand followers. What I consider a friendship is just good business for Ali. Yet, as I spend countless hours watching Ali's life unfold, I feel deeply connected to someone who does not know that I exist. This parasocial relationship* is the perfect recipe for loneliness and we've all tasted it. Let me remind you. If you grew up in the 1990's you'll recall that your bedroom décor was largely restricted to three poster options: option one was Michael Jackson from *BAD* in a black leather jacket, option two was Tom Cruise wearing aviator sunglasses in *Top Gun* or option three was Brooke Shields wearing, well, not very much at all. Going to sleep every night underneath

---

* Parasocial relationships are one-sided relationships in which one person is deeply invested while the other person doesn't know that they exist.

these posters made you feel like you had a bond with these celebrities, almost as if you knew them. 'Aha! That's a parasocial relationship,' a social scientist might say. But the difference is that it was easy for us to keep these bonds in context because Brooke Shields never spoke back. In today's world, where YouTubers, Insta influencers and gamers constantly interact with their fans, it's increasingly easy and common to think that there's a real relationship there. Unsurprisingly, recent studies show that teenagers worldwide increasingly report feeling lonely,[25] even in a period when their Internet use has exploded.[26]

This sense of disconnection seems to creep into our IRL friendships as well: we've all been sitting with a friend who absentmindedly starts checking their phone mid-sentence. You don't want to sit by idly, so you reach for your phone as well. Before you know it, you're two friends sipping coffee many worlds apart. A recent study showed that 89 per cent of cellphone owners used their phones during their last social gathering. Kids spend hours talking to their friends from the sidelines of a virtual game. Wedding proposals are vlogs with hashtags and married couples apologize to one another on Twitter. It seems that so many of our relationships—with family, friends and acquaintances alike—are now conducted at arm's length, and often with several people simultaneously. You post something on social media and immediately turn to say something in a WhatsApp group chat while responding to the ping of an email. Buried neck-deep in our phones, sacrificing quality for quantity, we march down a lonely road to isolation. We are more connected and yet lonelier than ever, and sometimes, it seems that social media had us social distancing well before the pandemic.

I'm speaking to a group of tweens from Bengaluru, all of whom recently got their own Instagram accounts. I ask them to describe their group's 'Insta rules' as they see it:

Rule 1: 'If someone comments on my photo, then I have to comment on theirs. And if they put up a birthday post for me, then I have to put up a birthday post for them, or they'll think that I don't care.'

Rule 2: 'Close friends have to comment on your post whether they want to or not.'

Rule 3: 'If you want someone to know that you're angry with them, don't comment on their post. Like they'll know that you've seen it, but you're purposely not commenting on it.'

Rule 3A: 'And not commenting is super important because when everyone sees that you're not commenting, they will know that you're not happy with that person.'

It's easy to start thinking of friends as numbers when birthdays become a running tally of how many of your friends posted for you and who put up a story instead of a post. A few years of this and it's easy to start a habit of *collecting friends instead of being friends*. Social media taps into our hardwired sense of social obligation and then stands back as we run around reposting and retweeting each other. Lost in this heady swamp of likes and retweets, it becomes harder to remain authentically connected, even though I know what you ate for breakfast, and you know where I went for dinner. Sooner or later, the loneliness comes home to roost, and we return to social media looking for connections. That's like an overweight man eating more doughnuts to fix his weight problem.

All of this distance comes at a cost: disconnected and disoriented, we're all drowning in a tsunami of mental health crises. Yet, the clue to solving these mysterious ailments couldn't be simpler. Harvard's definitive study on happiness, one of the longest-running studies in the world, reveals a simple truth: *If you want to be happy, stay connected.*

A Lesson from the Jamaican Bobsledding Team

In a world where happiness is often quantified by the validation of strangers, it's worth spending a moment being deeply truthful to yourself and encouraging the kids to do the same. Ask them to think about all the instances when they experienced true happiness—it likely had nothing to do with fake reviewers boosting their comment section or counting how many people posted stories on their birthday. Deep joy typically comes from moments of connection—with yourself and others—whether playing a board game with the family, laughing till your belly hurts with an old friend or enjoying a sunset with your fingers curled around a warm cup. We've all felt the pressure to capture that sunset for Instagram. It'll probably take twenty tries to get it right, and by then, the warmth of both the sunset and the coffee will be long gone. There isn't much joy in that.

All of this began to make sense to me on a recent Tuesday night. Tuesday is movie night at our house; we usually order in some pizza and curl up as a family to watch a movie. In a bid to introduce the kids to our old favourites, we picked *Cool Runnings*, the classic about the Jamaican bobsledding team that competes for an Olympic gold (the ultimate external validation). With everyone hankering after the medal, I watched as the coach told his team, 'A gold medal is a wonderful thing. But if you're not enough without it, you'll never be enough with it.' It was like he was saying to Gulshan, 'Yes, likes are great, babe. But no, likes aren't life.'

Social Media GPS: Empowering Kids to Find Their Digital Path

This devastating pandemic unexpectedly birthed some pretty incredible things. For one, young people all over the country took to social media to make kindness cool. They delivered food to senior citizens who couldn't leave their homes and used social media to encourage others to join the effort. As hospitals ran out of oxygen, the images of these young people became the life support that we needed. They weren't relief workers or humanitarian aid professionals—they were regular kids with a conscience who knew how to harness the power of the 'gram. Fifteen-year-old Naira taught herself to bake and delighted her Insta followers by announcing that she was donating the year's profits to a Covid charity. Nineteen-year-old Arshia started making personalized masks and posting about them on social media. She was soon flooded with orders and employed several out-of-work *karigars* to embroider her creations (her business is still active and the *karigars* are now fulltime employees). In an upscale south Mumbai building, a pair of brothers pledged to wash the residents' cars for Rs 100 per car and donate the proceeds to migrant labour camps. After they posted photos of their efforts on social media, several other kids in neighbouring buildings began taking out the washcloths too. Kindness was trending.

It wasn't just the kids; adults pitched in too. Psychologists conducted free Facebook Live sessions on coping with isolation and anxiety. Contact numbers for oxygen tanks and medical supplies were amplified by influencers across Instagram. During Delhi's devastating second wave in 2021, my friend Puja was desperate for an oxygen tank for her mother. The tank finally arrived because a stranger, Aman, drove across Delhi during a citywide curfew to deliver it. Aman's sister had recently been admitted to a hospital with Covid, and while waiting in the hospital's parking lot, he saw a friend's post on behalf of Puja's mother. Within minutes, he was driving across town with a tank that would ultimately help save a life. All Puja and Aman had in common was Instagram.

Social media, when used with a sense of purpose, can be an incredible tool for connecting people. Fifty-seven per cent of teens said they had made friends online[27] and that number will only have risen by the time you read this. Social media's unprecedented ability to connect ensures that most of us will never quit it, and, sooner or later, all our kids will be on it. But when is a good time to allow your kid to get a social media account? For starters, we would do well to remember that even Facebook thinks we should wait until the kid turns thirteen before letting them have their account.

The hope is that by then their brains will have developed some natural defences against the addiction. But once they have access to a private social media account, then what?

Almost as an answer, one of my WhatsApp parent group chats is pinging maniacally. My friend Shyla recently attended an online safety seminar for parents, and she's dumbfounded. 'Did you know the eggplant emoji means penis and lollipops mean "suck"? I didn't know that the two cherries together meant boobs and the two eyes together meant "send a nudie"!' The chat keeps pinging as other parents join in. One parent issues a warning about the Discord app. 'That's where the paedophiles hang out,' she says. As well-intentioned as this exchange is, it is ultimately pointless. Even the trendiest parent amongst us will eventually find it impossible to keep up with the latest slang, the coolest app or how to actually use Snapchat streaks. For my part, I often forget to update my apps and so staying current with iGen describing anatomy as though it were a fruit salad* seems like a tall order.

Social media companies know exactly how difficult it is for parents to keep up. In an internal presentation,[28] Facebook employees discussed teen mental health and noted that 'parents can't understand and don't know how to help'. I read that sentence several times, infuriated by this summary dismissal of parents. While we may have been born when dinosaurs walked the earth, there are certainly ways in which we *can* understand, and *can* help. Here's how to start:

---

* Cherries + peach emojis = Small tits, big ass

1) Begin the Conversation

If our children are digital natives, then we are digital immigrants. This might upend the traditional power balance in the parent–child relationship, but hey, immigrants can learn a great deal about their host country by simply asking the natives some questions. Asking iGen about their online worlds gives us an opportunity to understand this most private part of our kids' lives. Ask them about their favourite YouTuber or the Snapchat filters they're using. Chat about their *PUBG* game score or the latest TikTok challenge doing the rounds (hopefully the kids have stopped licking airplane toilet seats). Get to know which videos they like to watch, or whatever drama is unfolding in the comment section. At this point, your kid might seem like the expert while you're feeling like the country bumpkin. But wait, you're about to reclaim parental authority: tell them you've heard of Finstas* and aren't a fan! That should help you regain some ground! If they need more convincing to see you as a resource, consider reminding them that you have real-world experience. Ultimately, most of the drama in the comment section boils down to a few basic human emotions—envy, greed and fear. Even though you may not be hanging out in the comment section yourself, your lived experience makes you an expert in dealing with those emotions.

2) Get Uncomfortable

Providing an endless escape and frictionless experiences, phones disconnect iGen from the greatest teacher of

---

* If you haven't, quickly put down this book and look up Finsta.

all—discomfort. Their phones ensure that they are never alone and that can make them very lonely. Standing alone at a party and feeling left out? Watch Tiktokers take on the latest challenge. Feeling anxious? Scroll through Instagram (and inadvertently increase your anxiety). Want a break? Take a VR walk on Mount Fuji. Time to break up with your girlfriend? Simply type a few words, swipe delete and move on. Phones are omnipresent and ready to provide a convenient escape that cocoons iGen from any aches and pains. This is especially problematic because today's dark clouds are training grounds for life's eventual storms.

Humans are the only primates to have whites in their eyes, which helps us to follow each other's gaze and build deeper connections. When you see something joyful, I see it too, and we celebrate together. When your eyes fall on something sad, looking at it together helps us to share the sorrow. Humans were always meant to experience deep intimacy with one another, which includes working through difficult feelings. While the kids experiment with technology, they must also experience life. Teach iGen to put away the phone, look their friends in the eye and work through those annoying, uncomfortable feelings.

3) Don't Post Anything Grandma Shouldn't See

Whether it's a crazy night with friends that has accidentally found its way onto YouTube, a private photo that was forwarded without permission or a screenshot of a regrettable comment, the Internet never forgets. The vast majority of college admissions officers in the US say that it's 'fair game' to visit an applicant's social media pages to learn more about them.[29] From college admissions and job applications to potential love interests, remind your kid that everyone will first check them out online. Insist that they maintain clean accounts. Teach them about the importance of consent both while taking photos of other people and while being recorded themselves. 'Don't post anything on social media that you wouldn't want your grandmother to see' is a good thumb rule.

4) Especially for Girls

While both girls and boys are glued to their screens, boys generally spend more time playing video games[30] while girls spend more time on social media, specifically Instagram. But unlike video games which disappear when you close the app, Instagram follows you around. You agonizingly edit a photo to make sure it's perfect but the worry doesn't end after you've posted it. For hours later, you're constantly checking in, nervously awaiting judgement and fretting over the outcome. Instagram, unlike video games, requires public performance, something that young women often internalize. And sure enough, in this tsunami of mental health crises, it's painfully clear that teen girls are experiencing record levels of sadness and suicidal thoughts.[31] Remind the girls that Instagram is not reality. No one who is truly living their best life is focused on putting it online for strangers to validate. Explain the difference between narcissism and self-worth, and how #toocool4u is an example of the former.* Ask your daughters to explain their idea of

---

* Also, can we agree that, as grown adults, we should just stop writing #youcantsitwithus on our party photos?

physical beauty and pay close attention to see if they're leaning towards cyborg ideals. If they are, remind them that human bodies mirror our mortal lives that include the pleasures of hot chocolate, ice cream and vacations. No number of likes makes life worth not living. Besides, in the words of Taylor Swift, 'You are not the opinion of someone who doesn't know you.'

But even if your kid is active on social media, it's not all doom and gloom. Instagram recently revealed that its algorithm prefers content that doesn't appear to be Photoshopped, and it has banned 'plastic surgery' filters in an effort to make the platform a healthier environment.[32] Despite the platform's efforts, young people are well aware that Instagram is highly curated and many are craving something more authentic. Some are gravitating towards apps like BeReal where photos are unedited, unfiltered and given an asterisk if they were retaken. Photos taken outside of the two-minute time frame are marked with how late they were posted—a mark of shame, of sorts.[33] 'BeReal won't make you famous,' reads the app's description. For many kids not interested in being influencers but still voyeuristically interested in their friends' lives, this may be a good thing.

But we must do more. In an ideal world, apps and platforms would collaborate to minimize the harmful behaviour—the endless bullying, polarization and addiction to likes—that runs largely unchecked, especially on platforms that allow children. In a US Congressional hearing with the TikTok CEO, congresswoman and paediatrician Kim Schrier implored Big Tech for help.

'We need you to do your part,' she said. 'It could save this generation.' As things stand, the business models of most websites depend on attracting traffic, and they have no incentive to ensure that this traffic follows any sensible rules. In fact, many websites are incentivized to deliberately cause eyeball-grabbing accidents because let's be honest, who can look away from a train wreck? Scandals, slander and sex sell. Hatred and strong emotions make the app stickier. Far from bringing the world together, this is a recipe for fraying societal fabrics and fracturing the planet. And yet, that's precisely what's driving the world. Facebook employees have turned whistle-blowers, the US has held endless Congressional hearings, India has banned apps, EU regulators have attempted to break up hegemonies and everyone has written exposés. But none of this has worked. Tech is moving at the speed of light, far faster than any lawmakers and regulators can keep up with which leaves us parents as the last line of defence. We'll have to help ourselves and our kids navigate this web. And while we may not know exactly how NFTs work or the difference between Bitcoin and Ethereum, we have something far more valuable: our own untethered childhoods have given us the benefit of perspective. That's what we need to pass on to the kids instead of simply handing them the latest iPhone.

Drinking Responsibly: How Parents Can Guzzle Less Social Media Dope

Social media has turned everyone into a (potential) celebrity. The results have been disastrous but also highly pleasurable, not to mention massively profitable—a lethal combination[34]. Everyone, including 'real' celebrities, is complicit in this disaster, clamouring as they are for digital celebrityhood. Pope Francis created history by being the first pontiff to have an official Instagram account. Former US president Donald Trump insisted on a 'modern-day presidency' featuring his unique brand of midnight tweets. And one of the first things King Charles did after his mother's official mourning period ended was update his Instagram and Twitter profile photos. It's no surprise then that even the most present among us can't help but try out for those five minutes of online fame. While social media is often most intoxicating for its youngest users, adults can get drunk on dope too. This inebriation often has far-reaching consequences especially since the kids are constantly watching how we handle our drinks. Here are a few reminders to help you drink responsibly:

1) Curate Your Feed

During the summer of 2021, Covid risk was central to our family's decision making and we severely limited our social interactions. Forget about taking a vacation, even going out for dinner was quite literally off the table. I'm not sure whether it was lockdown exhaustion or just plain old-fashioned Instagram envy, but something snapped when I saw two of my girlfriends sipping poolside drinks and enjoying #summervibes while I was calculating vaccine efficacy rates. Unfollowing them seemed rude so I decided to use my old ally—the mute button. Muting someone on Instagram simply means that you will no longer see their posts. No, they won't know that you muted them, and yes, you can unmute them once sangria season is over. And just as you mute content that brings you down, make sure to follow accounts that lift you up. Find content creators focused on making cool, authentic content and remember to like a few of those posts immediately so that the algorithm can recognize your preferences. At this point in the human-AI relationship, we still have some control over the algorithm so take this limited-time offer to curate your feed and tailor your happiness.

Wresting back some control from the algorithm is more crucial than we realize. Big Tech's algorithms consistently create echo chambers around us, feeding us our own diets and amplifying polarization. They are highly topic-based, so if you express an interest in say, gardening or climate change, the algorithm picks it up and thrusts you into those specific worlds. The algorithm then influences everything by creating a filter bubble in which you only hear your voice and others like it. Think of it like this: instead of allowing you to roam free and wide in a bookstore, selecting titles of your choosing, reading a little of this and some of that, the algorithm kicks you out of the bookstore and then force-feeds you a reading list of its choosing. Instead of reading and exploring freely, you are forced into a one-dimensional marriage. Don't let the algorithm box you in. Attempt to read content on every side of the political spectrum. Turn off auto-play on YouTube and choose what you want to feed yourself.

2) Uncurate Yourself

It's easy to keep the fantasy version of yourself—the one that gets the most likes—alive on the Internet. You can filter your photos, airbrush the blemishes and reveal only the Instagrammable parts of your home. This may seem like you're playing in a funhouse of mirrors but performing for likes while boxing yourself into a curated projection has real consequences. It's difficult to feel good about your authentic self when you only receive validation for your digitally curated fantasy. What if you abandoned the idea of perfection and released yourself from the prison of public performance? Unless your business relies on social media traction, consider freeing yourself from panting after likes. Try posting without posing, share an unfinished project or a kitchen fail. Betray the idea of perfection, it's the only way to be true to yourself.

3) Try Intermittent Fasting

During Lockdown 1, when we were still checking in on each other's vegetable supplies and panic levels, my friend commented that her fourteen-year-old son was doing really well even as the world fell apart. 'All Aahan needs is uninterrupted Wi-Fi and a locked door,' she chuckled. But even after the lockdowns were lifted, Aahan remained holed up in his room, continuing to live his life online. 'I know he's feeling low, but he says that when he feels really low, he spends more time on his phone. I barely see him now,' his mother said. He isn't alone: many teenagers use the Internet as an escape mechanism until it becomes both the problem and the solution. *Dard bhi aur dava bhi.*

This addiction is both real and rampant. In fact, the problem is big enough problem to have forced social media platforms to add tools that limit your time on their platforms. Allowing moderation is a good start since addiction experts such as David Sheff point out that digital addiction is less like alcohol addiction (in which you try to abstain completely) and more like food addiction, in which moderation is key[35] (you've got to eat to stay alive). You're likely familiar with intermittent fasting in which you abstain from food for several hours a day—digital detoxes aren't very different. Your best bet to conquer a digital addiction is with balance and boundaries. Start with small, achievable goals such as going off social media for the weekend and build from there. If a whole weekend is too much, use productivity apps like Freedom to lock yourself out of social media during certain times of the day. Managing your time on these platforms is tough but ultimately worth it: piles of research demonstrate that the less you use social media, the less depressed and lonely you feel.[36]

4) Don't Scroll, Connect

Remember that it's not just how much time you're spending on social media that affects your well-being, but also *what you're doing there*. If you are mindlessly doom-scrolling—looking at photos of strangers on vacation, reading catastrophic headlines and skimming viral videos—then you're setting yourself up for, well, doom. The business model of social media is based on 'people looking at content from as many people as possible, whom they may not know, for as many hours a day as possible'.[37] Don't contribute to the model—the companies are rich enough as it is—and instead reclaim control. Limit your time on social media and while you're there, use it to *actually connect* with others. Facebook's research[38] (they know they have a problem!) reveals that *people who actively use social media are happier than those who passively consume content*. These platforms were originally designed to be networks and our well-being depends on staying true to that original intent. So, leave a positive comment, message an old friend or engage with people who share your interests instead of passively doom-scrolling through cat videos.

5) Live IRL

Everyone appreciates a compliment. We all enjoy the thrill of recognition—to be noticed when we're looking good or to feel credited for a job well done. Receiving feedback is a fundamental part of the human experience. It's part of the reason we buy new clothes, improve our diction and apply lipstick. But being insular IRL affects our traditional feedback loops by forcing us to forage for feedback online, hunt for likes and conflate them with value. We're seeking validation online because we're living less offline. Break the loop—go out, engage with people, push for real-world experiences and receive the feedback that you're craving. Multiple studies have found that the best predictor of social and emotional health is face-to-face communication. The studies are right—no heart emoji can replace the dizziness of a first kiss just as no clapping emoji comes close to the pride of walking up to a stage to receive a trophy. Texting 'LOL' is not the same as actually laughing across a table with an old friend. You can do a digital puja and put a virtual blanket on a dargah but that cannot replace the communal, meditative aspects of prayer. Besides, the real world is the only place you can get a decent meal.

CHAPTER THREE

NAKED AND IN LOVE: REVEALING IGEN'S DIGITAL DESIRES

Sex and the Screen City

Nikhil, nineteen, is filling me in on what just happened with his girlfriend. 'I know she was upset, but I replied nicely. Then she got angry, then her best friend got involved and then she got *really* angry.' It's a very absorbing story but it takes me a while to realize that none of the events that Nikhil describes ever happened face-to-face. I clarify and he pauses to look at me quizzically. 'It's the same. Why does it matter if it was online or not?' he asks, sounding annoyed. He's right; it doesn't really matter. Not to Nikhil, anyway.

Nikhil and I met over lunch at Delhi's Khan Market. Sitting there talking about Nikhil's jilted girlfriend jolts another memory. Almost ten years ago, my friend Pranav wanted to break up with his then-girlfriend and decided to break the news to her over text. A decade ago, it seemed cold and impersonal, almost cruel to break up with someone over text. Today, none of that matters: declarations of love, regret over breakups, apologies for transgressions and promises of forever are all carried out on chats, DMs and the sidelines of virtual games. As iGen comes of age, they do so with both hands firmly clasped around their phones. Through several interviews with tweens and teens, it was evident that many in iGen have embraced virtual dating. Or as they call it: dating.

For those of us who grew up with a dial-up connection, it's difficult to fathom a romantic relationship that is entirely online. Then again, most of us grew up with struggling modems and ICQ while iGen has 5G and the metaverse. While some iGen agree that a physical interaction provides an incomparable connection, many of those I interviewed believe that virtual dating works just as well. They have good reasons:

'It's so much easier, fewer things to coordinate, there's no traffic.'

'You can't get her pregnant on a virtual date.'

'It's way cheaper than a real date.'

But with all its conveniences—no traffic, no restaurant bills, no shocked shopping for diapers—virtual dating brings its challenges. I'm talking to fourteen-year-old Shreya, who says she would never cheat on her boyfriend.

Not that he is her boyfriend.

Wait, is he her boyfriend?

The Viber messages aren't clear.

She's not sure if he's her boyfriend.

Just like Nikhil broke up with his girlfriend over WhatsApp, Shreya is (possibly) getting asked out on Viber. Teenage relationships have always been bewildering but now, riddled with DMs and posts stripped of facial expression or body language, they can be cryptic even for iGen. Rishi, sixteen, says, 'Everything involves texting. No one calls anyone anymore. But texting . . .

it's a different language. It's so easy to get something wrong and misunderstand someone. And if you're misunderstood, you're going to get cancelled for sure. Either by a few people or many but it's going to happen.' To avoid being misunderstood, Rishi adds emojis to every text. Not that emojis are foolproof—their meanings are constantly changing and often need careful dissection. I am fond of using the thumbs-up emoji to signal that I am in amicable agreement with something, but I was recently informed that many folks consider this emoji passive-aggressive. Even sarcastic. I'd apologize with a joined palms emoji, but I've just been informed that's a high-five!

In the years when they should be practising what it takes to develop meaningful relationships, iGen often has to spend hours reading between the lines trying to decipher a message or a post with a hidden meaning. While it's tempting to dismiss these early relationships as 'puppy love', they're hugely instructive, setting the blueprints for our self-worth and how we will treat others. That awkward moment of figuring out whether or not to lean in for a first kiss is actually a critical lesson in reading non-verbal cues, arguably one of the most important skills humans ever learn. Operating in the virtual realm, our kids explore their sexual identities in a different way, often without touch and sometimes bereft of intimacy.

Bakul Dua, a clinical psychologist, says that preteens and teens are now 'experiment[ing] before they can even understand intimacy and its consequences.' Bakul, who has worked in schools in Mumbai and Bengaluru, seems to be on to something—the Internet has invented a new normal, especially when it comes to exploring sex.

From watching porn to sexting your partner or having an anonymous sexy chat online, digital sexy is the norm for many iGen. Most have seen a digital gang bang before they've even had a chance to hold someone's hand. Online is where many tweens and teens experience their 'first times'. Gone are the days when you spent time alone in your bathroom with some faded, stolen magazines. Chaturbate.com and other websites now invite you to chat while you do your thang.

I spend an afternoon with Krisha, seventeen, and two of her friends, all of whom will leave for college soon. I'm telling them about a new study that says 62 per cent of women in India actively sext.[1] The girls agree that sexting has always been a big part of how they explore intimacy. 'It could be anything. Like you take a sexy photo of yourself and send it to your boyfriend,' says Krisha. 'Maybe he can't reply right away if he's with the fam or something, but he'll reply soon.'

'What would he send back?' I ask.

'Probably another photo or maybe a request. Depends on the vibe.'

None of the girls use WhatsApp for their intimate chats, preferring the added security of Telegram and Signal which include features like disappearing messages, secret chats, no forwarding and an immediate notification if the other person takes a screenshot. Sexting, like IRL sex, could last minutes or hours and seems to bring them comparable euphoria. 'It feels the same as IRL,' says Gunjan, one of Krisha's friends, 'sometimes it's even better because you send something and then you can see the double tick and then you see "typing . . .". The anticipation is also really sexy. And you can get fun and creative with photos and emojis!' The girls are right. Emojis are a big part of how iGen does sexy, with 72 per cent of young adults saying they find it easier to put their feelings across in emojis than in text.[2] Aside from eggplants and peaches, the girls teach me a lot that afternoon:

Rain (the three droplets) is what follows when the eggplant and the peach spend some sexy time.

Fist emoji + water droplets emoji = masturbation

Tongue-out emoji = oral

Ok hand emoji = anal

Peace sign emoji = vaginal

Alongside emojis, teens have also developed their sexting shorthand, including CU46 (see you for sex), GNOC (Get Naked on Camera) and NP4NP (Naked Pic for Naked Pic). Irregular for many of us, this is standard fare in the lives of most teenagers with a phone and perhaps rightly so. Consider this: if this technology had been available to you as a teenager, wouldn't you have tried? Teenagers have a naturally strong sex drive with everything being so enticingly new. They are newly beautiful, all these interesting parts of themselves newly emerged, the freedom newly earned, the hormones newly released. It's intoxicating. And sexting with its instant gratification and inherent risqueness is equally enchanting. It's practically made for the teenage mind! In fact, Snapchat was born because its then college-going founders were enchanted by the idea of disappearing nudes.[3]

This is not to say that sexting is easy for parents of teenagers. I am supposed to meet my friend Rashmi and her teenage daughter Trisha as part of my interviews. Rashmi shows up without Trisha because the mother and daughter aren't currently on speaking terms.

A few days ago, Rashmi installed a camera in Trisha's bedroom which has obviously irked Trisha. 'I'm so scared that she's going to take her clothes off for some boy. She's only fifteen. I can't see what's happening on her phone, but with this camera at least I'll be able to see if she starts stripping,' Rashmi says, her voice shaking. I ask what prompted this sudden decision. 'She lied to me and told me she wasn't on TikTok. Then a teacher was being bullied online, and Trisha's TikTok account was involved. That's how I found out what she's been up to.' Rashmi went from blissful ignorance to militant vigilance overnight and for her part, Trisha hasn't spoken to her mother in a week. For my part? My heart breaks for both of them. More than a heartbreak emoji can show.

In an attempt at consolation, I remind Rashmi about the upsides of virtual intimacy: iGen are physically safer than they have ever been. STDs and teen pregnancies are at an all-time low globally. In the UK, the teen pregnancy rate has declined by over 55 per cent, with researchers jubilantly touting this as the success story of our time.[4] This success is mirrored globally and research suggests that it is the rise in sexting that has helped lower the teen pregnancy rate.[5] That's good newsworthy of several celebratory emojis!

And even for those unconcerned about getting pregnant, finding sexy communities online is often a liberating experience. Perhaps one of the most powerful social urges we have as humans is the need to belong. With its unrivalled ability to bring people together, tech creates a sense of belonging for those who often find themselves sidelined in the mainstream. I spoke to Leila, a queer nineteen-year-old who has recently come out to her family. 'I only had the guts to do it after my online community encouraged me,' she says. This sentiment is common among many iGen whose sexual preferences or identities fall outside the cis-het square. Especially for those living in homes where queerness is still a caricature, going online to find belonging has become essential.

Your One and Only, Online

More than any other age group, teenagers crave constant connection. While many teens connect with each other, some will head to the pros to find intimacy. In a world that is online 24/7, connecting with a pro has never been easier. Consider onlyfans.com, one of the tech industry's hottest unicorns. While the site does not focus exclusively on adult content, it is massively popular with sex workers. Predictably, OnlyFans exploded during the pandemic, going from a user base of seventeen million followers in 2019 to over 120 million users today. An OnlyFans fan describes the site like this: 'Think of it as Instagram for porn. Except that if you like what you see, forget about the "like" button, you can ask the influencer to do something especially for you, right there and then.'

Danii Harwood is a popular influencer on OnlyFans, and her job is to make you feel special. She makes it her business to know what her fans like, their desires and their dreams. And she will do what she can to make those fantasies come true. On Mistress Mondays, Dani will dress like a dominatrix. On other days, she'll be a shy schoolgirl. As the *New York Times* reports, 'He may pay her to help him achieve an orgasm, though she is not a prostitute. He may purchase erotic videos from her, though she is not a porn star.' Regardless of whether she is brandishing whips or pigtails, Danii's job is to make you feel intimately close, almost like you're in a relationship with her, she will give you that 'girlfriend experience'. Her clients come away thinking intimacy *matters* to her. 'Things happen so quickly online,' says Elaine Ducharme, a psychologist who specializes in cybersex addictions. 'Some people really begin to think the other person is in love with them. They develop this intimacy and fantasy relationship. The cool thing about fantasy relationships is they don't require any work.'[6]

For kids who are coming of age online, who have never experienced intimacy in any real way, Danii's 'girlfriend experience' can be distorting. Yes, they know that the fantasy isn't real, but the suspension of disbelief is part of Danii's job. How are you ever going to be satisfied by your IRL girlfriend when you can have the fantasy of Danii Harwood instead? An object retains its fascination if it keeps changing and retains its sense of novelty. As every married couple knows only too well, human partners cannot keep reinventing themselves endlessly. But guess what can? Online fantasies. As the American Psychology Association says, 'Your primary partner will never be able to compare with the fantasy partner. They will never win.'[7]

Is Virtual Sex Really Sex?

Whether it's the fantasy of Danii Harwood or the sexting that iGen favours, some might contend that virtual intimacy isn't real. After all, is it even sex if you aren't physically touching your partner? Kavita, twenty-five, would reply with a resounding 'yes!' I spoke to Kavita, who has been 'living and loving' on Second Life for years (well before Zuckerberg announced the metaverse). On Second Life, people create avatars that 'have a second life in an online virtual world'.[8] As its creators have repeatedly stressed, Second Life is not a game; it is intended to mirror life itself. There is no set objective, no medals to be won, these are avatars just living their lives. On Second Life, Kavita's avatar is married to Ginny's avatar. Their avatar wedding was attended by their avatar friends, who came to celebrate them and pass on their good wishes for their marriage. Later, when Kavita and Ginny moved into their brand-new virtual house, their avatar friends came over with flowers, dinner sets and other housewarming gifts. I ask Kavita whether she thinks her online life—including her sex life— with Ginny is real. 'It's very real to me,' she says emphatically, 'just because it's online doesn't make it any less real.'

Many young people seem to agree with Kavita and a new study reveals that two-thirds of young people plan to continue being just as virtually intimate as they were during the pandemic.[9] Whether it's video chats, sexting or phone sex, as iGen takes sexy online, there is an entire industry that supports them. Krisha draws my attention to the 'Jibe', a Bluetooth-enabled vibrator[10] that she has been using with her partner for a few months. She inserts the Jibe, and the app allows her partner to control the vibrator's speed and tempo from wherever he is. 'Sex doesn't always have to be face-to-face,' Krisha says with a laugh. After all, this is a generation that goes for a movie on Friday night, spends Saturday afternoon sexting one another before meeting for a dinner date and then wakes up on Sunday morning to Jibe.

As Nikhil might say, what's the difference?

Porn, Unlimited

For most of us, our first experience of porn was a hastily stolen magazine sneakily enjoyed and then returned with great precision to its original spot underneath a dusty mattress. My colony* friend reminds me that our neighbourhood video-*bhaiya* would hand the boys a naughty DVD surreptitiously hidden in a brown bag with a knowing wink. Far from being a private act, watching pre-Internet porn was a community experience. In fact, it cemented many friendships. During our last year of school, several of us bunked classes to watch a 'blue movie' in a seedy theatre in Delhi. Although the movie title is long forgotten, the raw headiness of that day—of being embarrassed and excited in equal measure—has lived on for decades. Before XXX data streaming, watching porn required planning, smarts and the ingenuity of similarly motivated friends. Today, there is an endless supply of sexy available around the clock. No planning needed;

---

* Because Delhi's imperialist hangover isn't acute enough, we often call our neighbourhoods 'colonies'.

it's all available on a private device that can slide out of your pocket whenever the urge strikes. India was already one of the world's largest consumers of pornography, and then online porn reported a 95 per cent spike during the lockdown.[11] Let's just say that online porn in India doesn't need Viagra: it is permanently and defiantly up.

We have achieved porn on tap.

Most of our kids are consuming porn earlier than we think. In the US, 'porn' is the fifth most popular Internet search word for kids aged six and above.[12] That's not a typo either. In India, the average age for viewing porn for the first time is ten[13] and it is getting younger. None of us—not even the most committed tiger parents—has the time to block all the porn ever made from our kids' phones. And even if we misguidedly tried, the truth is most porn filters don't work[14] anyway. Most tweens don't go looking for porn but first come across it accidentally. I spoke to Kavya in Mumbai, who said that she and her friends have received 'random d**k pics' on Tumblr and Snapchat since they were eleven years old. A ten-year-old boy tells me that he was dared by his classmate to Google 'sex', and then, predictably, curiosity took over. A friend reports that her son discovered porn while doing a science research project for school. 'He was doing a research paper on echidnas [spiny anteaters] which are monotremes [unusual egg-laying mammals] and therefore have unique penises [the penises have four heads]. He clicked on one weird site and it opened up a whole world of porn,' she says. I shudder and try not to imagine what the algorithm delivers when it thinks you're interested in discovering 'unique penises'. But echidnas or not, sooner or later, porn is bound to enter your kids' online world. Whether deliberate or accidental, kids see online sexy all the time, and pretending it doesn't exist is insulting your kids' intelligence. More importantly, it's a waste of your time. No matter how vigilant you are as a parent, be assured of two facts: your child will come across something inappropriate online, and it will likely happen earlier than you think. Even researchers are struggling to map the implications of this phenomenon because—I kid you not—it's difficult to find control groups of children that aren't watching porn![15] So given that our children are test subjects in a giant social experiment with no control group,* we may as well roll up our sleeves and figure out how we can help. It's time to unfasten your chastity belt and get ready for a crash course—we have a lot of bumpy ground to cover!

Porn is accessible, anonymous and affordable. Actually, that last word was just for alliteration—porn is often free. Consequently, many iGen boys are streaming porn before the alarm clock rings, watching golden showers before they shower, watching multiple orifices being eaten as they contemplate breakfast and watching gang bangs on the bus to school. Want to watch someone masturbate? Head over to chaturbate.com which provides live webcam experiences 24/7. The site boasts over two lakh registered performers, many of whom leave their cameras on all the time. Users can also turn on their cameras for some two-way sexiness. As Sid, nineteen, a (self-professed) porn connoisseur told me, 'Unlike sites like stripchat.com that pretty much force you to pay, on Chaturbate you don't

---

* In the history of the world, no generation has grown up with 24/7 access to free, hardcore, high-definition porn.

even have to tip the girls if you don't want to. And there are always so many cam girls [on Chaturbate] that it's just a great free place to chill and get horny.'

Sid spends a great deal of time on Chaturbate; 'it's my favourite site,' he says. But he concedes that it's not always practical to have videos on: 'especially during lockdown, my parents were always home, so it was safer to just be on chat sites.' I ask what he usually uses for sexy chat sites. 'Reddit is great for that kind of stuff—there are so many great subreddits like r/IndiansGoneWild, it's awesome! But there is no data privacy on Reddit, so many of my friends use apps like Dust or Telegram, which basically make your messages turn to dust in a certain time period.' I get it: Dust is basically the digital alternative to returning the naughty magazine to the dusty mattress—it erases your footprints.

Porn is an industry backed by Big Data, and to retain its pole position, it constantly evolves with changing technology. Online porn provides endless menus for our kids to choose from; there are as many porn sites as there are stars in the galaxy. The competition is fierce; each of these sites must compete for attention and therefore constantly offer up something fresh and exciting. They have to elicit desire, not yawns, and so the porn industry works hard to offer features (HOT NASTY KINKS CAM TO CAM!!!!) and access (FREE!!! NO SIGNUP NEEDED!) that hold our kids' attention so that they don't click away. Much of this includes offering fetishes that you never knew you wanted—from midget porn to bestiality, nothing is off limits anymore.

Bestiality and midget porn notwithstanding, it might be relevant to pause here and remember that there's nothing inherently wrong with pornography. Pornography can be an icebreaker, a mood enhancer, a much-needed lubricant and sometimes all of those things at once. During the pandemic, it provided hours of respite for millions of people battling loneliness and depression. Porn is not a civilizational threat and in itself, porn does not erode women's status; think about the countries where pornography is banned—Saudia Arabia, China and Pakistan—they're not exactly countries considered torchbearers for human rights.

Porn is fine, even great, when responsibly enjoyed by adults who understand that it is a performance. When understood as fantasy or entertainment, porn can be fun and kinky, even liberating. Millions of adults across the world enjoy porn and say it has helped bring sensuality into their relationships. However, these are grown-ups who have had the benefit of experiencing physical intimacy, in all its sweaty, awkward and very real ways. Many of our kids have not, and so the pervasiveness of porn—its everywhereness and allthetimeness—has serious implications for them. It's difficult for us to fathom how pervasive and *persuasive* porn is in the psyche of iGen, especially boys, because none of us grew up with porn on tap.

Learning How to Drive from Vin Diesel

Porn is something you actively participate in, you rock to it's beats. It often elicits a primal response and when a young boy finds his phone flooded with hot images, his mind and body engage with that content in a visceral way. Studies[16] across the world reveal that most young people today explore porn before they explore other people implying that their first expectations of bodies and sex come from porn. But here's the thing: porn as sex education is like a trapeze artist teaching your toddler how to walk. Porn is often the circus version of sex, where everything is fast (women orgasming on cue), furious (loud, jackhammering, pummelling sex), and fabulous (hairless, perfectly toned women purring with a come-hither look). But most of us aren't Cirque du Soleil performers. As adults know, intimacy in real life is often clumsy and awkward with several fumbling attempts before you get it right. The clumsy efforts, laced with affection and romance, are often the part that partners will remember for years. None of this— what makes human sex real and mutual—has a place in high-octave mainstream porn, where a man goes from delivering pizza to cunnilingus in minutes. Online porn makes sex seem effortless as though everyone *just knows* what their partner wants; from women's privates to men's moves, porno sex is always smooth. Adults realize that this isn't true, but iGen's inexperience lets them believe in the fantasy.

Science terms porn as a 'supranormal stimulus', which is basically a fancy way of saying that porn floods your brain with more perceived pleasure than normal sexy stimulation. Very quickly, porn can become sexier than sex itself. It's like this: imagine if the first time you discover the taste of orange is through orange candy. What a lip-smacking sweet–sour flavour! Gosh, it makes your tongue sizzle! You enter a candy store and find unlimited varieties of this orange candy—orange candy covered in sugar, orange candy with sticks coming out, pointy orange candy, rounded orange balls and orange candy paired with other candy. And it's all there waiting for you, unlimited, free of charge, whenever you want. Now imagine that you've been lost in the delights of that candy shop for months when you encounter a real orange for the first time. It's imperfect and inconvenient; it has weird spots and this tough outer layer that you have to peel off just to reach the fruit, which then has peels and seeds. It takes so much work—the pleasure isn't readily available. And when you finally get to the flavour, it seems bland despite all that work. You're so used to the bazooka flavour that orange candies provide that a real orange tastes boring. Just like sex after a steady diet of porn.

Perhaps porn star Tasha Reign summarizes it best as she talks about what happens when kids learn about sex from porn: 'Adult filmmakers make content for adults. We are entertainers,' she says. 'We fulfil a fantasy like Vin Diesel fulfils a fantasy. You wouldn't want to learn to drive from Vin Diesel.'[17] But that's just it—around the world, our kids are learning to drive from Vin Diesel! And just like *Fast & Furious* makes seat belts and speed limits inconsequential, porn often dispenses with safety and consent. Condoms, the most basic premise of safe sex, are completely absent in mainstream porn. Instead, flashy pop-up ads for trends such as ATM* are standard on porn sites. Apparently, hepatitis is sexy these days.

This is the first generation to experience puberty with access to 24/7 porn and it will be a while before we

---

* Now if you think ATM is a cash dispensing machine, it's time to climb out from under that rock. A stands for Anus and M stands for Mouth. I'll leave you to do the rest of the math.

can fully map their experiences. For many, however, the opinion is already out. In a BBC interview, former adult film actress Mia Khalifa agreed that porn is damaging relationships in a corrosive way. 'Of course it [porn] affects relationships,' she says. Social theorist Jackson Katz says that to believe that porn has no effect on children is to be 'wildly naïve in the twenty-first century. To think otherwise is to live in a fantasy world'.[18] And yet, we continue to be wildly naive. We've landed on the moon, but there aren't many reliable offline places where a kid in India can learn about sex. I ask Nandini, fifteen, from Chennai about her sex education class in school. 'It was nothing,' she says with an embarrassed laugh. I persist; I'm eager to know what happened. 'Well, Ma'am [the biology teacher] separated the class into boys and girls. Before she started, she said that there was strictly no laughing allowed. Even if one of us laughed, she would close the chapter. No laughing and no questions. Then she talked about the different body parts.'

'Like what?' I ask.

'Like scrotum and fallopian tubes.'

Versions of this story were repeated with children I interviewed from four Indian cities. The National Education Policy (NEP) has no mention of sexuality, while 'sex education' is timidly named 'adolescent education'. Even as the decades march on, sex education in a majority of our schools still focuses on scrotums and fallopian tubes. No laughing, no questions. India isn't alone: 60 per cent of students in the UK turned to porn to find out more about sex.[19] Students in Hong Kong are watching more porn than ever before, but reports indicate that their knowledge of sex has declined.[20] And with a decline in knowledge comes a widening information gap in areas including consent and safety.

Porn is Performance

Sex may be about pleasure, but porn is about camera angles. 'Having real sex is totally different than having porn sex!' says porn star Charlotte Cross in a video interview.[21] 'Everything that we do is for the people back home who are watching it. Something that looks good to you guys or to somebody watching me doesn't necessarily always feel the best for me,' she continues. Adults might enjoy watching a performer scream in an XXX video, but they know that real lovemaking can be quiet, even silent. Watching someone being repeatedly flipped like a pancake on a griddle may be entertaining but even porn stars don't always want those acrobatics in real life. 'No one has sex in the positions that we shoot in,' says[22] porn star Arabelle Raphael. Interviews with porn stars consistently reveal that performers are asked to 'cheat out' to the camera to make acts that may be painful in reality appear pleasurable on screen. Charlotte's colleague, Sasha Heart, another porn superstar agrees: 'You're just doing a performance. *That's* the word I want to use—you are *performing* sex.'

Many porn scenes have a checklist of acts that need to be filmed before the day's shoot is done and checking them off this list is the actor's job. The performance can be gruelling for male stars as well. In a deeply personal interview, Lance Hart, a veteran male porn star agrees, 'Deep throating is not always awesome. If a girl's going down on you for a scene, she's going to be at it for a long time . . . eventually you start feeling molars on the head of your d**k. Getting paid to receive oral sex is basically like getting your d**k chewed on for an hour.'[23] One performer estimates that it takes four hours of work to create a ten-minute porno.[24] Others say it could take longer with several porn shoots lasting twelve hours at a time. Since it is impossible to maintain erections for this long, many performers use pills, injections and surgeries to get the job done. 'Most of our male talent uses some form of medical aid to stay hard,' says porn star Kayden Kross. 'That can be anything from Viagra to Cialis to injections that will keep erections going without arousal. I know others have had surgeries to implant penis pumps.'[25] That might explain why porn stars seem like they can doggedly do the deed for days while in reality, 75 per cent of men ejaculate within three minutes.[26]

As any professional will tell you, porn is hard work; it takes experienced actors, trained crews and professional equipment to make sex look that sexy on camera. Despite the obviously performative nature of porn, the line between reality and fantasy is increasingly blurred for young people often creating feelings of confusion and debilitating inadequacy. Through these interviews, I've spoken to scores of iGen who are completely willing to suspend belief and think of these performances as real. In the absence of any real conversation and experience, porn becomes the tutor. Instead of fantasy, porn becomes sex ed.

Get your Freak(Tok) On

In June 2020, a young girl named Kiara uploads a TikTok video[27] that receives over thirty-five million views.

'Decided to watch *365 Days** with my guy friend,' she coos, and then the camera pans to her body: there is a deep black–purple bruise spread across one of Kiara's thighs matched by bruises and what look like burn marks on her other thigh. Her arms are similarly battered, accompanied by burns and cuts all over her body. She ends the video happily, signing off with a smile and a peace sign. While Kiara's post is popular, it is not unique: *365 Days* sparked a massively popular TikTok trend with young women all over the world flaunting their cuts and strangulation marks. Depending on how much you've unfastened your chastity belt, you might consider paying a visit to #freaktok, a subversive corner of TikTok where choking and beating video challenges are the norm. With content creators competing to shock and entertain, vanilla sex is quickly becoming boring. On TikTok alone, #ChokeMe has over forty-five million views.

Despite what the neighbourhood video-bhaiya handed over in that brown paper bag, it's safe to say that things have never been this hardcore in any generation. Globally, teens watch significantly more hardcore porn than their same-sex parents. Boys aged fourteen to seventeen are three times as likely as their fathers to have seen double penetration, gang bangs and facial ejaculation. The differential between girls and their mothers is even higher. I am speaking to seventeen-year-old Vrinda from Mumbai. She and her boyfriend Akash have been watching porn together since they started dating. 'Sometimes, we would watch together at

---

* *365 Days* is a Polish erotic thriller that became one of the most successful Netflix movies of all time.

someone's place. Sometimes, we would send each other stuff to watch when we were alone.' They would send each other photos of porn stars whose 'vibe' they liked. 'He would dress up too, so I didn't feel like I was doing it alone.' It all seemed edgy and sexy but safe. 'It was the first time for both of us, so it was like we were in it together,' says Vrinda. Then Akash suggested they try choking. It dominated the porn that he had been watching and seemed too sexy to resist. The couple experimented with it, but Vrinda wasn't convinced that she liked it. 'I tried it, but quickly said "no". Of course, he stopped immediately but later he started sending me photos and videos of couples doing it. It was a lot of pressure. Plus, all the girls looked like they were really loving it. I thought maybe there's something wrong with me,' she says.

Erika Lust, one of the world's few female porn directors, agrees that strangulation scenes now dominate porn. 'Face slapping, choking, gagging and spitting has become the alpha and omega of any porn scene and not within a BDSM context,' she says. 'These are presented as standard ways to have sex when, in fact, they are niches.'[28] Gail Dines, an expert in the study of pornography, believes the normalization of violent sex in mainstream culture is very real: 'Hypersexualised media and porn work to groom young people into internalizing the belief that "rough sex", is normalised, legitimate and an accepted form of sexual play. Boys learn this from media, video games, and mainstream hardcore porn, and girls use porn as a guide to what boys and men want.'[29] Many of the young women I spoke to suggested that they were struggling with similar themes: the pressure to be good at 'non-vanilla sex' and to say yes to what they see in porn. Perhaps that's why Akash couldn't understand why Vrinda refused—all those women in all those videos never once said 'no'.

None of this is about kink shaming. And anyway, the Internet did not invent sexual kinks; kinks and niches have been around ever since humans started playing with one another (and themselves!) In fact, kink communities, including the BDSM community, can teach us valuable lessons about consent, dialogue and mutual respect. As those experienced in BDSM reiterate, the practice is rooted in communication and emotional maturity. Unfortunately, those aren't the pillars holding up the online porn industry today. All of this is complicated by the fact that these videos are being watched by people who are too young and inexperienced to understand the difference between sex positivity and violence. TikTok, where Kiara uploaded her *365 Days* video, welcomes users from the age of thirteen. Far too young to see shades of grey.

Harder and Harder

Everyone's WhatsApp blew up simultaneously in December 2019. A group of furious parents reported a WhatsApp group chat between a group of fourteen-year-old boys who attended the same elite school in south Mumbai. Within hours, parents all over the city were reading the transcripts of the chat, and it didn't matter if you had a son or daughter; everyone's hair collectively greyed overnight. SexGate was here.

'I'll destroy that little b**ch,' said one boy.

'Should I go full on and kill her existence?' replied another.

The idea of raping their classmates was a running theme. The boys wanted to 'bang', they wanted to 'gang bang' and it was clear that the girls (their classmates since kindergarten) were dispensable. In fact, they were 'trash'. In one exchange, the boys discuss which of the girls they would prefer 'for a one-night stand'. 'Then one night we just go and bang her,' concludes one of the boys.

Newspapers, TV channels and parents banded together in shock and outrage over the chat. While the outrage was understandable, the shock seemed naive. Think about it: our children, especially boys, consume a steady diet of violent porn on a regular basis. From aggressive fucking to face slapping to brutal anal 'punishment', the porn that many boys are being exposed to is hardcore XXX content. Before many teenage boys even brush their teeth in the morning, they have watched a woman being choked, gagged and slapped. 'At that young age, you don't really know what's what and you just follow whatever you see on porn sites,'[30] says a teenager. Rape videos are innocuously called 'local films' and sold on street corners for a few hundred rupees. A shopkeeper selling these 'local films' insists that 'porn is passé. These real-life crimes are the rage'.[31] An estimated 40 per cent of the young men in Goa watch 'rape porn'.[32] Why then are we surprised by descriptions of rapes and gang bangs on our boys' WhatsApp chats?

Teenagers have always imitated what they see on screens (it's why we all wore baggy jeans and awkwardly tied our shirts around our waists in the 1990s) and iGen is no different. Kids are often clueless, especially at the beginning of their sexual journeys. As a curious tween, a nine-year-old boy might do a simple Google search to see what's out there. He may type in 'boobs' but what he sees next is extraordinary and well beyond his understanding. Once a young boy is catapulted into this world and watches a video or two, the algorithms are only too happy to help. He will soon find an endless supply of hardcore violent porn, slapping, beatings and choking as far as the eye can see. Porn aggregators, like Pornhub, use self-reinforcing algorithms like the rest of the Internet, so once your content history is established and you've watched one gang bang, the algorithm is bound to serve up more. It's the same algorithm that always has the perfect video from your favourite movie star lined up as 'Recommended for you' on YouTube or shows you advertisements of brown handbags just when you tell your friend that you are looking for a brown handbag.

Back to the porn. Watching porn creates the typical downward spiral common to many addictions: the brain quickly gets desensitized to even this supranormal stimulus and you need more hardcore stuff (and larger quantities of it) to achieve the same level of pleasure. *Dil maange more* and obviously, the porn industry is right there to give you more. Mainstream porn is brimming over with videos of 'gang bangs' cut to a shot of a woman being raped, while a man calls her a 'dirty slut', pulls her up by her hair and pushes her head down to his penis: the classic 'blow me off, bitch' scene. Pain and humiliation are standard fare. Studies indicate that 88 per cent of mainstream porn features men in acts of physical aggression while the targets of the aggression are overwhelmingly female with most showing pleasure when treated aggressively.[33] So when a young boy, with no other sexual experience, watches a woman being repeatedly raped, it makes him believe that physical aggression is fun for everyone. Girls like it. But 'what porn constructs as a fantasy, in the real world is often rape, sexual assault and abuse'.[34]

Multiple[35] research[36] studies in the US studies reveal that adolescent boys who watch sexually aggressive porn are more likely to be sexually violent. In the UK, reports[37] state that the availability and normalization of extreme pornography have led to a dramatic increase in the number of young women experiencing unwanted slapping, choking, gagging or spitting during consensual sex. While research of this kind is largely unavailable in India, experts anecdotally point to a similar trend. The men who raped Nirbhaya were watching violent porn before they raped her. Now, this certainly doesn't mean that every boy who watches violent porn will want to rape a woman. That would be a gross oversimplification. But it does point to a concern that as sex gets increasingly 'pornified', iGen is soaking up a toxic, violent stew without any context for this content. In a country like India, where the sexes are still segregated and sex education is practically non-existent, a diet of violent porn with no other context for sexual interaction could be disastrous.

The girls that were being discussed in SexGate were scared of going to school. No girl anywhere in the world should be afraid of going to school. Malala has taught us that much. But take a closer look at SexGate and you might see that we also need to worry for the boys. Mainstream porn culture has them simmering in a stew that is saturated with stereotypes of dominance and aggression with no place for consideration, let alone rejection. All over the country, our boys are growing up in a culture that instructs them to always be rock hard, massive and manly. That men should be demanding and degrading since humiliation is standard. But perhaps most damagingly, it teaches boys that girls will respond to aggression with pleasure. Porn is ushering in 'an incredibly brutal form of men's sexuality'.[38]

We owe our daughters a better world, but SexGate made me realize that we owe it to our sons with the same urgency. I was discussing this with my friend who has two young sons. At the end of the conversation, she looked at me, misty-eyed, and asked, 'So are the boys victims too?' We're so hardwired to think of girls as casualties that we never stop to consider our boys. To me, SexGate was a cry for help. This time by the boys.

Just How Naked: Managing Porn in Kids' Lives

Roblox's Lego-looking avatars and cheerful graphics are so inviting that it's no surprise that two-thirds of all US kids between nine and twelve use the platform.[39] Every other tween in India seems to be on it too. The site is so popular that at the time of writing, Robux—the site's digital currency—is worth more than the Russian rouble. But even in this kid zone, there's plenty of NSFW content, including condos where avatars meet to have sex. One Roblox scene features a 'naked man, wearing just a dog collar and a lead [being] led across the floor by a woman in a bondage outfit. Two strippers [dance] next to a bar. A group has gathered around a couple openly having sex, watching and occasionally commenting'.[40] All this in a world purpose-built for kids.

Sex is all over the Internet, and it underscores a basic premise: we cannot block out all sex-related content from our kids' online diets. Sites like Roblox are constantly trying and failing—just as soon as they take down one sex condo, another one pops up. It's like trying to drain a river with a kitchen sieve. And just as we can't block all sexy content, we certainly can't monitor our children 24/7. The camera that Rashmi has installed in Trisha's room is ultimately pointless; in fact, teaching Trisha to make better decisions could offer her better protection. Better decisions are needed because, in many ways, iGen has it tougher than any generation before them: hardcore porn is available on tap, #slutchic is trending on Instagram and everyone seems to be sexting everyone else. As parents, it's time to stop with the cameras and start with the conversations.

1) Let's Talk about Sex, Baby

I am over forty and married with two children, but my parents still squirm when the s-word comes up. While researching this book, I asked my mother why she had never had 'the Talk' with me when I was younger. 'I didn't want to spoil you,' she said plaintively. *Spoil me?*

This unwillingness to talk about sex was echoed by many of the parents I interviewed, all of whom have teenage children. The reasons ranged from embarrassment ('I don't know what to say.') and cultural silence ('No one talks about it. My parents didn't talk to me either.') to outright fear ('She'll start thinking that sex is okay. I don't want her to become *that* kind of girl.'). The panic underlying these responses was perhaps best summarized by the mother of a fifteen-year-old boy who said, 'I'd rather cut off my head than talk to him about sex.' At 1.4 billion people, we clearly know how to do it, but we'd rather chop off our heads than talk about it.

This deafening silence comes at an enormous price and more often than not, it's our kids who have to pay. Our silence means that our kids lose the chance to turn to infomed people who care about them. Instead, iGen turns to the Internet, and—I hate to break this to you—the Internet doesn't care about your kid's well-being.

If you're waiting for your child to turn thirteen before talking about sex, it's likely that porn will get there before you. We've got to talk early and clearly because, despite their overt squeamishness, the kids often want us to have this talk with them. Older teenagers recently created a guide to help parents with this issue, and the overarching message was clear: *talk to your children about sex-related issues before they get a phone.*[41] Young children have no context for sex and aren't naturally embarrassed by it which can make the conversation less awkward. Even if your kid has grown past the 'where do babies come from?' stage, the Talk is still necessary. Be prepared with resources, answer questions honestly and make sure your kid knows that you are always available. At this age, you'll likely get the eye roll when you begin the Talk. You might get told that the Talk is stupid. And boring. Totally unnecessary. But despite the eye rolls, the kids have never needed our help more: a staggering 92 per cent of surveyed Indian youth said that at some point, they had done something risky online.[42] Having the Talk is far from stupid; in fact, it might be the one thing that *keeps* them from doing something stupid. If you must have your kid turn to the Internet for sex ed (although you really should do it yourself!), then direct them to sites like www.amaze.org which will educate them better than Pornhub.

2) Pornhub Is Not Sex Ed

Contextualizing porn is not moral policing, it's a matter of public health. Our children, especially the boys, can quickly lose track of what is normal, given that they live one click away from women getting beaten, gagged and spat on. The hardcore violent porn that assaults our children makes conversations about consent and coercion absolutely critical. Yet, studies show that 88 per cent of college-aged boys—even in cosmopolitan cities like Mumbai—have received no sex education from their parents.[43] So just as we have the Talk early, we need to have the Talk clearly.

Pornhub was the technology company with the third-greatest impact on society in this century, after Facebook and Google but ahead of Microsoft, Apple and Amazon![44] I read that statistic a few times as I grappled with its implications. With this outsized reach, Pornhub will eventually enter your kid's universe. Take the opportunity to explain that Pornhub is entertainment, not sex ed. All women are not surgically enhanced, toned and hairless nymphs just like real men aren't all ripped jackhammers with XXL appendages.[*] Porn also creates unrealistic expectations about female behaviour; women are often presented as submissive recipients who are 'up for anything' which puts debilitating pressure on young women to succumb to every demand, no matter how demeaning. And since actors are routinely checked for STDs,[45] condoms are basically non-existent in pornos.

---

[*] Porn star penises are 6–9 inches long while the average male is 30 per cent smaller.

But in reality, communication about consent and safe sexual practices is critical: condoms will keep you alive and you're not uncool if you don't want to be constantly choked by a dog collar. To us, these may seem like obvious differences but to an adolescent whose primary sexual influence is online pornography, the lines are often blurry.

Given these ambiguous distinctions, iGen cannot absorb the Internet with eyes wide shut. Any porn with children, anything that resembles rape, anything with animals—you get the drift—shouldn't be viewed because it's almost always exploitative of those on screen. While ethical porn is available on the Internet, allowing your kid access to 'mummy-approved porn' may be too radical for many of us! What we can do instead is have conversations so that iGen understands that what happens in pornos doesn't usually happen on a regular Tuesday night with someone you love.

Sure, there are studies that don't find negative associations with consuming vast quantities of porn, but these studies have only reviewed adult participants. iGen is a social experiment unto themselves. A few drops of rain won't get your kids wet but a constant downpour will drench them. Today, it is simply pouring porn, and as they grow, more longitudinal research is needed to understand how porn affects iGen's self-esteem and intimacy with others.* We don't know what the future looks like but this much is certain—it is knocking

---

* That is, if scientists can find control groups that don't watch porn! A porn study at the University of Montreal, among others, was recently scrapped after experts failed to find any young men who had not watched porn.

at the door. Porn, some believe, has the potential to turn iGen completely off sex if left unchecked. As Gabe Deem, founder of the porn addiction community Reboot Nation says, 'You could have a whole generation of people that literally have to watch other people have sex on screen to be able to have sex with a real person.'[46] Best-selling author of *The Subtle Art of Not Giving a F*ck,* Mark Manson agrees; he had to go off porn for sixty days to resolve his sexual performance issues. In a research article titled 'Porn Can Ruin Your Sex Life', Manson writes: 'Researchers debate whether or not porn addiction is a real addiction but . . . the semantics don't change the fact that many people experience real problems with porn. It's been implicated in things like unhappy and unsatisfied partners, as well as depression, anxiety and loneliness.'[47] A new study conducted by the European Association of Urologists puts it more bluntly: 'The more porn a man watches, the more likely he is to experience erectile dysfunction during sex—even if he's young and healthy.' Many young boys struggling with porn-induced performance problems can feel isolated. They deserve to know that they can take back control. Research websites like www.yourbrainonporn.com and community forums such as www.rebootnation.com can help.

3) Challenge Yourself as a Parent

Whether porn, virtual dating or chat rooms, the Internet will likely figure prominently in your kid's sexual journey, especially early on. Is online infidelity considered infidelity? Does having sex online count as having sex? Perhaps it does, after all, the brain is the biggest sex organ, governing everything from arousal to orgasm. Then again, perhaps 'real' sex needs 'real' touch. This means that as parents, we will also be challenged to think about intimacy in previously unthought of ways.

This is a new world for most of us, so far removed from the issues of our childhoods. It can be disturbing to think that the device your kid uses to text their grandmother is the same device that takes them to a troubling, often twisted universe. The best way to untangle things is to have a straight talk. And finally, after you've had the Talk multiple times, dismantle the spy camera and allow iGen to make their own decisions, knowing that ultimately that is the only decision you can make.

CHAPTER FOUR

CATCH ME IF YOU CAN:
UNCOVERING CYBERBULLYING

Bullies Under Every Bridge

When I worked at UNICEF over a decade ago, one of the agency's largest departments had the all-encompassing title 'Child Protection'. Always bursting with energy and unlike other departments that focused on intractable, systemic problems, the folks at Child Protection often seemed to be dealing with urgent issues: rehabilitating a group of children sleeping at the Kochi railway station or rescuing girls facing harassment at a traffic light in North Delhi. Their phones seemed to be constantly ringing with critical calls to action, and I recall the department springing to respond with equal urgency. Child Protection still exists but now the department has added a new focus—*online* child protection—and commissions large-scale reports on cyberbullying. To me, this is a telling shift by one of the world's largest child welfare agencies; it highlights that urgent protection is needed not only for hungry children sleeping at railway stations but also for well-fed kids sitting in their air-conditioned living rooms.

Today, they are all vulnerable.

Kids vs. Kids

Remember that age, usually around fifteen or sixteen, when you felt like music had been written just for you? It was the age that had *all the feels*; songs pulled at your heartstrings and every emotion was felt so deeply. Growing up in the 1990s and hearing Meatloaf croon *I Would Do Anything for Love* meant staring rapturously across the classroom at your newly pubertal crush and wondering what the two of you might do together one day. It was around this time of raging hormones and mixed tapes that a nasty rumour went around my school about Sheila S. Apparently Sheila had gone 'all the way' with Rahul K. She had done *that*. Gasp. In the weeks that followed, a group of girls would shadow Sheila, loudly singing Madonna's *Like a Virgin* in direct reference to her newly minted status. *Touched for the very first time.* Decades later, I still can't listen to Madonna without thinking of Sheila's face, all dark shadows and hurt.

It wasn't just my school. My editor, Shreya, tells me about how the Head Girl at her school was caught giving head to her boyfriend. You can imagine what followed. 'That's why she's *Head* girl!' and 'You give such good head, girl!' went the comments. Decades later, Shreya still remembers the charged atmosphere in school during those weeks.

If Shreya and I remember these incidents as bystanders, I can only imagine how haunting they remain for Sheila and Head Girl. But there is a silver lining: Sheila and Head Girl grew up in an analogue world which meant that the taunts didn't follow them home. When school ended for the day, they could leave it all behind, at least until the next morning. If Head Girl was a teen today, she would run the risk of her private moment being recorded in perpetuity and beamed from data centres in Singapore and California as it popped up on the screens of every kid and teacher in the school. It would be inescapable no matter where she went. Today, everyone has a smartphone, which means everyone has a broadcasting device.

Disha, sixteen, tells me about a recent incident at her school in Mumbai. A group of five girls had been close friends for several years, sharing sweaters and secrets in equal measure. Loyalties shifted when their section changed, and the once inseparable group slowly began to drift apart. A few months after the section change, posts started going up on the anonymous messaging site ask.fm for the whole school to read. Every post had damaging information about each of the five girls. ONE says that she's a virgin but that's not true. TWO'S dad regularly cheats on her mom. THREE likes girls even though she's dating a guy. FOUR will meet you in the senior school bathroom for a blowjob. FIVE tried to kill herself. The posts were intensely damaging and so deeply private that it had to be one of the girls posting about herself and her friends. But who? The posts went up even when all five girls sat in class with no devices. I interrupt Disha as she tells me the story, it sounds like the plot of a teen Netflix show! 'Yeah, but it happened in front of us,' she says. 'We never found out the identity of the poster, but it got so bad that the school had to hold a special assembly. They banned ask.fm from the whole school. No one in the school was allowed to have an account anymore.' Ask.fm is a popular anonymous messaging site that many students describe as 'toxic' and 'poisonous', and while the ban might have been laudable in its intent, it was ultimately ineffective. 'We just moved to other sites like Whisper that the teachers didn't know about,' says Disha.

Trisha's story and Sheila's as well as Head Girl's experiences highlight an interesting fact that I came across in my research: studies[1] on cyberbullying indicate that meeting a harasser online is not the biggest risk, the real problem is often what *our kids do to one another*—the bullying, the intimidation, the whispers and the comments. In many instances of cyber harassment, *children are both the victims and the offenders*. If your child is on social media, chances are that they have either witnessed online harassment or worse, even perpetrated it: UNICEF reports that 43 per cent of Indian children active on social media witnessed cruel behaviour, while 52 per cent of children had bullied others themselves.[2]

When you connect the dots, it leads to a frightening realization: the numbers indicate that between your home and mine, it's likely that one of us is raising a cyber bully. As are most of our friends. Aashika, fifteen, is a dear friend's daughter—one of those kids I've known since she was in diapers. Now far too grown-up for lullabies, Aashika tells me that she recently created a Musical.ly chat group and deliberately left one girl out. Let's call this girl Excluded. Over the next few days, Aashika and her friends ran a concerted social media campaign that had two specific features: 1) All the posted photos had to show the group having fun and 2) Everyone in the group had to be in every photo without—you guessed it—Excluded. The campaign led up to a finale event—a party to which Excluded wasn't invited. The group of girls then individually sent Excluded forwards of the party invite with the identical caption: 'To Miss Crazy Hair. Stop trying to be our frnd. Cant u see how much we all hate u.'

Phones offer endless playgrounds of manipulation where trouble is easily stirred up and while Aashika acknowledges her problematic behaviour, it's clear that with a typical teenager's immature prefrontal cortex, she doesn't fully understand the consequences of her actions. Our brains develop from the inside out and from the back to the front implying that during the teen years, the fastest firing part of a teenager's brain is the part responsible for emotions and the least developed is the frontal lobe responsible for thoughtful decisions. If lack of impulse control is a hallmark of the adolescent brain so is the desire to fit in with peers. Teenagers are hardwired to follow one another like flocks of birds. No sooner has one bird raised its wings to fly, the rest of the flock is in the air too which explains why Aashika's friends followed her cruel lead. Together, they created a situation that will likely haunt Excluded for the rest of her life.

While excluding people is not a new social phenomenon (most membership clubs are premised on some notion of exclusivity), the difference now is that social media turns exclusion into a gladiator-style spectator sport that never turns off. It used to be that when you went home from school, on vacation, or the weekends, you were off the hook. But now, Excluded is always excluded, regardless of time or place, because Aashika and Co. are always on. For many kids on the receiving end, cyber harassment is a bottomless bowl of bullying in which you are constantly and very publicly drowned.

'I Haven't Deleted It, and You Can't Make Me'

The stories continue to abound, and this seems like a chapter that will write itself for all the wrong reasons. A friend connects me to her younger cousin, Shailee, nineteen, a confident young woman who recently broke up with her boyfriend and went on to deal with the aftermath. 'He [ex-boyfriend] knew all my passwords. A few nights after we broke up, I realized that he had hacked into my Facebook account. First, he changed my display pic to a turd. Then he switched it to a really suggestive pic of me in a bikini, a photo that I had sent him when we were together. Soon he was posting updates on my account, pretending to be me and saying things like "Hi, I'm Shailee. I'm single and horny. My boyfriend left me, and I want to get laid so bad",' she says quietly.

'But surely everyone would have realized that this isn't you posting?' I ask.

'Yeah, many of my friends realized that my account had been hacked. Still, it was the worst few days of my life—so many of my relatives are on my Facebook. I felt totally helpless,' she replies.

Despite the trauma, Shailee thinks that she ultimately lucked out. 'He has some photos of me that should never, ever get out. At least, he never posted those on Facebook.' I ask Shailee if she has since asked her ex-boyfriend to delete those photos. She has. 'What did he say?' I ask. 'He said, "I haven't deleted it, and you can't make me."' And there it is—nine words that instantly transform into the nine circles of hell. *'I haven't deleted it, and you can't make me'*. All too often, we mistakenly assume that our online dealings are private, that WhatsApp chats will remain confidential, or an intimate photo will stay a secret between two people. Shailee is far from alone: studies suggest that one in ten ex-partners threaten to expose risqué photos online—a threat that is actually carried out more often than not.[3]

As Internet connectivity penetrates our farthest villages, even rural India is contending with the vulnerability of being circulated online. In a shocking incident in Bhirbhum, West Bengal, the local panchayat decided to punish a sixteen-year-old tribal girl for falling in love with a non-tribal boy. She was stripped publicly and made to walk around the village while the village men harassed her and took photos of her naked body. These videos and photos were then circulated in the village as a warning to other girls.[4] I decided to Google this incident in an effort to understand it better. What I found instead was XXX sites selling adivasi girl videos: 'adivasi sex village girl mms real' at XNXX.COM, 'adivasi girl outdoor sex MMS caught by a voyeur' and several others. The search results catapulted me back to the Delhi Public School MMS scandal that rocked our capital city in 2004. It's been two decades since that incident. In those decades, we've found the God particle, built robotic hearts, edited genes and 3D-printed food but somehow, *somehow*, we're still selling illicit videos of teenage girls on the Internet.

Nothing Trends Like Trolling

How are generally polite and well-meaning folks—people like you, me and our children—capable of such cruelty? Why do we intentionally exclude some people, blackmail others and betray the trust of those we once loved? Evolutionary biology might hold a clue. Growing up, remember how your parents would remind you to make eye contact when you spoke to someone? 'Look people in the eye,' they would insist. Well, it turns out there was a crucial reason for that: looking someone in the eye activates your limbic mirror systems, allowing you to reflect the other person's emotions. If they feel happy or sad, our neurons fire to mirror that sentiment. This simple act does something enormously powerful: it creates a bond. However, as an increasing number of our activities from grocery shopping to birthday parties move online, life loses its texture. We lose opportunities to create empathy and perhaps that's why Stanford neuroscientist Jamil Zaki insists that in today's world, *empathy itself is becoming endangered*. 'Online interactions often replace living hangouts and by comparison, are thin and bloodless . . .' he notes.

It's easy to see how these brittle interactions can make our empathy fragile too. Blackmailing your ex is relatively straightforward when you can do it online, and it's much easier to taunt your classmate when you don't have to look her in the eye. Similarly, it's effortless to spew hate speech while huddled behind a screen. As digital vigilantism takes over the Internet, there is a new casualty every day. The rest of us watch wide-eyed as keyboard warriors destroy even the most unassailable personalities for some perceived insult. The original crime is inflated until people are cancelled, careers are lost, and reputations besmirched. We're living in a world where 'everyone alive is either cancelled or about to be cancelled'.[5] Most of us feel helpless in the face of this 'cancel culture' and so we look on dumbfounded as online mobs mete out punishments that are often disproportionate to the original crime. Cheered on by their flammable protests, digital mobs take on a life of their own, spewing violent speech with a flippant disregard for the truth as they burn down everything in their path. Hiding behind the protection of their screens, trolls think nothing of telling someone to kill themselves or move to a neighbouring country. Trolling is twice as popular as positivity[6] and so perhaps it's no wonder cyberbullying is always trending. Today, it seems that there is a troll living under every virtual bridge.

Empathy Unleashed: How to Cancel Cyberbullying

Indian parents are in a unique position. Many of us are culturally conservative folks who refuse to talk to our children about online safety living in a country with appallingly low conviction rates for Internet-related crimes and yet we have the highest mobile data consumption rates in the world.[7] Strangely, we do have a precedent for this odd situation: it's akin to how we refuse to talk about sex but somehow ended up with one of the world's biggest populations! Humour aside, this deafening cultural silence and low conviction rate make for a volatile situation highlighted by a frightening statistic: India has one of the highest rates of cyber harassment worldwide.

Monica Lewinsky (remember her?) was Patient Zero of the cyberbullying scourge and says that she was the first person whose global humiliation was driven by the Internet. Lewinsky was twenty-two when the scandal broke, and two decades later, she is still defined by the stain on that blue dress. She is now driving a campaign to make the Internet a more humane place by asking some valid questions: when does this culture of humiliation become too much? And how do we support the Internet's youngest users—our children—to filter through this smorgasbord of anonymous cruel posts, whispers, yikes, tweets, pokes and torment?

Luckily, there is plenty we can do.

1) Build Your Toolbox

Building a toolbox of safe online practices is key to creating safe online experiences. Teach the kids to cherry-pick the people they follow and encourage them to keep their accounts private, a simple act that allows them infinitely greater control over their followers. If they have a public account, consider having them filter the information they release and as a policy, never mention their live location or address. If they are speaking to strangers online (and they probably are), encourage them to interact with an unknown person publicly first before letting them slide into DMs. Teach them to never accept and normalize abuse—a rude or creepy comment should result in an immediate block. Having these conversations and helping them build their toolbox is more effective than limiting their choice of platforms.

2) Know the Law

Recently, in a university hostel in Chandigarh, a first-year female student allegedly filmed secret videos of her female classmates in the common hostel washroom with the intention of circulating these videos. According to the chargesheet, the student was under pressure from a man with whom she had shared compromising photos of herself. He was blackmailing her with these photos and demanded nudies of other women in the hostel.[8] Essentially, she was taking compromising photos of others because of her own compromising photos. While the investigation was underway at the time of writing this book, it's abundantly clear that the matter only came to light because other students demanded action. This makes sense. If iGen is to live in this digital world, they will have to learn how to protect themselves in it. While India has a long way to go in terms of developing implementable cyber harassment and digital privacy laws, there is no need to assume that a cyberbully cannot be brought to justice. Provisions under Sections 66 and 67 of the Information Technology Act are particularly helpful and include:

- Penalties for publication and transmission of obscene material, material containing sexually explicit acts, and material depicting children in sexually explicit acts.
- Printing, selling or advertising grossly indecent or scurrilous matter or matter intended for blackmail.
- Making sexually charged remarks is considered sexual harassment.
- Violation of privacy.
- Criminal intimidation by anonymous communication.
- Sending defamatory messages by email.

The uncomfortable truth is that as parents, we can't be certain whether our children are being bullied or are cyberbullies themselves (remember that 52 per cent of Indian children admitted to bullying people over social media). Regardless, awareness of the law is crucial.

2) Become a Resource

While talking to iGen for this book, I came across one too many kids who, after facing bullying online, turned to strangers in a chat room for comfort, assuming they would never find support at home. It's a dangerous idea— having a vulnerable child lurking in chat rooms looking for a shoulder to cry on. If your kid frequents anonymous sites, it's important to ask them to explain their reasons. Perhaps they are dealing with a difficult issue and looking for a safe space to talk. Become that safe space, especially around topics of sexuality and bullying. Many of these topics are uncomfortable, but resources like 'So You Got Naked Online', funded by the European Union, can help (https://swgfl.org.uk/assets/documents/so-you-got-naked-online.pdf).

3) Push for Change

Social media sites are among the most profitable companies in the history of the world. Given that they are making money off our data, it's not unreasonable to ask that greater social responsibility be embedded in their business models. Almost all social media allow children and should be in investing in more 'switched on' moderators and better reporting tools. After all, many of the titans of the Internet, including Larry Page, Mark Zuckerberg and Parag Agarwal, are parents too. The product design built into each of their super successful products is based on behaviour modification, and surely, they can be applied to persuade users to behave better. Sometimes, all it takes is a simple feature; for example, an anti-cyberbullying app witnessed 167 per cent increase in kids sending encouraging messages to one another just by controlling when they received digital rewards like virtual confetti![9]

Sooner or later, companies must be financially incentivized to be involved in social change. The signs are already there—FB stock fell by 8 per cent[10] when the company was seen as not doing enough for the Black Lives Matter movement in the US. This is a good sign. The Internet is no longer distinct and separate from the physical world; the lines have now blurred. We all live online, and it's long overdue for the Internet to be managed as thoughtfully and with as much accountability, as our roads, schools and hospitals. If we don't allow bullying in our homes and schools, why should we stand by as it happens online?

4) Never Forget that Google Never Forgets

Mia Khalifa, one of PornHub's most popular performers, says she didn't mean to become a porn star. 'There's millions of girls who film themselves having sex and no one knows who they are, no one knows their name. I wanted to do it [porn] as my "dirty little secret". It blew up in my face,'[11] she says. Mia's words ring true: teenagers are often impulsive, sometimes even reckless.

This recklessness, especially if it involves the Internet, can have far-reaching consequences. Almost a decade after her first video went viral, Mia says that she still suffers from post-traumatic stress disorder, 'When I go out, the stares I get, I feel like people can see through my clothes. It makes me feel like . . . like I lost all right to my privacy because I'm one Google search away.'

Mia is not alone; each of us is one Google search away.

Generations of parents have comforted their children by saying, 'Hey, everybody makes mistakes. That's why you have erasers on pencils, right?' As parents of iGen, we've lost the ability to say that to our children. Gone are the days when we used pencils that could be rubbed out with erasers. iGen is using indelible writing instruments to document their lives. There are chat logs on every device; every word can be recorded and retrieved; each photo can make it across the world in seconds. You may think of your device as being personal, but it is public and permanent. Anything can become a billboard and deleting something means nothing because the Internet always remembers.

Fortunately, there are simple things iGen can do to reduce their risks of becoming Internet casualties, especially when it comes to intimate moments. First off, only engage in online sex with someone you would have sex with IRL. If you don't trust them with your real body, you shouldn't trust them with images of it. If your teen is in a serious, committed relationship, sending intimate photos might seem like a natural extension of that trust. It's worth reminding them that people change, and promises can be broken. Once you send an inappropriate photo, you lose all control over where that photo might end up.

This is especially relevant for young women as guys will often use pressure tactics for photos. Standard ploys include: 'Everyone does it, what's the big deal?' 'Tina always sends me pics.' 'I bet you look phenomenal with your top off. Send me a photo.' Even if iGen is comfortable sending intimate photos, it's still crucial to be cautious. Features like Telegram's Secret Chat are helpful since they forbid forwards and notify you if someone takes screenshots of your chats. Avoid sending images that contain identifiable features including birthmarks and scars, and never, ever include your face. Some teens I spoke to use apps like ObscuraCam to blur out their faces. Encourage iGen to know what's what: threatening to non-consensually publish photos is punishable under Indian law. This means that even the suggestion of revenge porn is a criminal offence. And while we're here, we should stop calling it revenge porn. That gives porn a bad name. We should call it what it is. As a prosecutor recently said, 'This is virtual rape.'[12]

CHAPTER FIVE

DOWN THE RABBIT HOLE: IS THE INTERNET MAKING US DUMBER?

What Was I Looking For?

Luckily, Darshan and I generally agree on which Netflix shows to watch. These are critical decisions and I'm grateful for this spousal harmony that has saved us years of strife. But even as the two of us relax to watch a show, the truth is that there's usually a third party in bed with us.

His iPad.

Darshan will watch Netflix while skimming the news on his tablet, his eyes and ears flitting constantly between two visuals and two volumes. 'Ask me a question about either show,' he'll say defiantly, convinced that he can keep up with both plotlines. And that's at night when he's more 'switched off'. During the day, he has two phones on him at all times, with multiple tabs open on each. On more than one occasion, we've sat down at the dinner table, and he's looked at me glassy-eyed, weary and almost delirious from the multiple screens. 'You do remember my name, don't you?' I once asked, only half-joking. His engine is on overdrive, and who knows when names might become too much.

He's not alone, I feel the pull too. Often, my phone doesn't even need to ping, my hands reach for it as though being pulled by magnets. Even when I unlock my phone with a predetermined intention, for instance, to reply to a particular email, something else invariably happens. I spend some time on today's Wordle. I get a WhatsApp. I reply to it. I stop by Insta to check my likes. Insta tells me that Justin Bieber has facial paralysis. I check on Justin. I get another WhatsApp. I reply to it. I go back to my Wordle for a few minutes. I go online to look for eczema creams and find a video of a hippo that took care of a turtle. I watch hippo videos for a while. WWILF, I think to myself. Or What Was I Looking For? Flying about somewhere in that maelstrom is an email reply that should have taken five minutes to write but which has taken fifty. Plus, I'm now exhausted.

We live in a post-speculative world. Google has all the answers, which means that we don't ever need to speculate about anything. Is your shirt grey or gray? What is the calorie count of a donut? Wait, is it spelled doughnut? What's the capital of Liechtenstein? When was the Hellenistic period? What's the crossbreed between a donkey and a zebra called? Just shout out 'Hey Siri . . .' and Siri, always on, always responsive, will end the speculation. But as the Internet—that shiny treasure chest of answers, decisive ender of speculations and supreme decider of arguments—gleams brighter, *are we humans growing dimmer?*

Changed Circuitry

I remember reading about the Flynn effect in college. Buried neck-deep in books and classes, it was heartening to read that improved access to nutrition and better schools had made humans smarter in the twentieth century. Perfect grades seemed more achievable—after all, we had all become collectively smarter! That buoyancy, however, lasted just a few short decades. As things stand, the world is experiencing a reversal of the Flynn effect, and global IQ scores have dropped precipitously by six points. The truth is, we're all turning a bit doltish. As one expert puts it, 'People are getting dumber. That's not a judgment; it's a global fact.'[1]

Most of us experience this doltishness every day. It's getting harder to remember the names of colleagues, words stay permanently suspended on the tips of our tongues, and really, who can remember anyone's birthday anymore? The Internet has fundamentally altered the way we process information, and as a result, we're all struggling to focus. Every time we go online, our brains get subtly rewired. And since we are online *so much*, our brains are constantly adapting to accommodate the Internet's deluge of small, shallow fragments of information.

Nicholas Carr, one of the most influential thinkers of our times, is the author of *The Shallows: What the Internet Is Doing to Our Brains*, which went on to become a Pulitzer Prize finalist. 'I'm not thinking the way I used to think,' says Carr. The Internet, he says, 'is chipping away [the] capacity for concentration and contemplation.' Online activity, especially when we're restlessly ping-ponging from one activity to another makes us lose focus. Jumping from text to email, opening one tab and then quickly clicking on another, switching frantically back and forth between news and notifications—all of this destroys the calm brain and creates a new kind of mind, one that becomes comfortable processing information in quick, fragmented bursts. The faster, the better.

As Carr's book title implies, over time our brains lose the ability to go deep. *We start living in the shallows.* 'Once I was a scuba diver in the sea of words. Now, I zip along the surface like a guy on a jetski,' he says. Admittedly, living life on a jetski sounds like great fun but you are likely to encounter a few problems. With all that wind in your hair, salt in your eyes and the world whizzing by, it's difficult to make thoughtful decisions. It's tough to stop and deeply appreciate beauty on a jetski or to meaningfully engage with an intractable problem. Given that our circuitry is so malleable, the more we stay online, the more we train our brains to be distracted. We can rapidly process snippets of information, but sustained attention becomes massively challenging.* The longer we are on the jetski, the more challenging it is to get off it.

It's not just Carr; scores of experts agree that the human brain simply wasn't built for the endless game of ping-pong tantalizingly offered by our phones. The consequences seem especially disturbing for iGen which is growing up with easy and immediate access to information which ultimately has an effect on how the kids function, both emotionally and otherwise. Experts suggest that this generation will have 'a thirst for instant gratification and quick fixes, a loss of patience and a lack of deep-thinking ability.'[2] 'Screenagers' are not the only ones affected. Nine and ten-year-olds indulging in over two hours of screen time per day scored lower on thinking

---

* Honestly, it's a marvel that you've made it this far into the book. Thanks for sticking around.

and language tests. Some kids saw a premature thinning of the cerebral cortex as they spent time on screens—their grey matter was disappearing.[3]

Disappearing grey matter or not, it's hard to stop! Regardless of which generation we belong to, none of us can stop pinging. Every notification, every distraction is a little dopamine nugget in disguise and it's challenging to focus on something when you're used to getting a reward hit every few seconds. Drunk on dopamine, we start liking the distractions. We seek them out. The more we seek them, the more we click and the more we click— bullseye!—the more accurately the algorithm can place irresistible links directly in our fields of vision. Think about the last time that you went to a shopping mall. You likely had a salesperson come up and ask you to try a product. It's usually not a big deal because you're likely to only encounter a couple of pushy salespeople per mall visit. But when you're online, the push and pulls come at you from all directions:

'Have you tried this new recipe?' Potatoes, green onions and a touch of mustard.'

'Are you looking to lose ten kilos in twenty days?'

'Have you checked out the season's hottest filter?'

'Become a millionaire overnight. Join our mailing list for just Rs 199'

'Join our community to always feel happy.'

'Free shipping on this summer's hottest perfume that will make you smell like Italian lemons.'

'Are you bored? Lonely? Depressed?' Here are fourteen essential oils that you need right now.'

'Looking for love? There's a big surprise waiting for you.'

'Get discounted Diwali hampers when you order in March.'

The sales push doesn't end because whether it's essential oils or real estate, the algorithm knows what we want better than anyone else. So, we click on these irresistible links, breaking our attention, disrupting our concentration and creating an avalanche of lost focus, which in turn, overtaxes our brains. And wouldn't you know it, an overtaxed brain finds distractions more distracting, and there it is: a self-perpetuating dependence loop. We click and lose focus, which makes us want to click all the more. Clickety-click we go all day, tappity-tap we go all night, leaking data and losing focus all the while.

You Can't Multitask, Not Really

'Effective multitasker.' Every employer wants one, every employee wants to be one. Darshan insists he *is* one as he attempts to wield multiple devices each buzzing and pinging with their miscellaneous tabs and apps. In reality, though, asking humans to effectively multitask is like squeezing water from a stone. We aren't built for it. Ever clicked on a tab, replied to an email, turned on Netflix, checked WhatsApp and then forgotten what tab you had opened in the first place? WWILF, you ask yourself. Or ever felt like you're forgetting everything and that your brain seems broken? Yeah, that's you sucking at multitasking. Join the club.

The more you multitask, the worse you get at what you set out to do in the first place. As modern phones effortlessly become integrated supercomputers, slot machines, porn portals, date finders and messaging services, it gets harder to stop multitasking. Sherry Turkle, a clinical psychologist and MIT professor, has students with their laptops open during her lectures, many of whom are simultaneously on messaging apps, YouTube and shopping sites as they sit in her class. 'I, and several of my colleagues, notice that the students whose laptops are open in class do not do as well as the others,'[4] she says. That's because Sherry's students are attempting to do something that is largely impossible (even for MIT kids): the human brain cannot perform two separate activities simultaneously with sustained focus.

The word 'multitasking' implies that you can do two or more things *simultaneously*, but in reality, the human brain constantly *switches* between the different tasks at hand. In moments where students think they're multitasking by simultaneously watching a video and listening to a professor, they're actually switching from YouTube to class and back to YouTube again. The trouble is that these switches are not seamless, each switch costs the brain a few moments to adjust. Those moments add up, especially when we're switching back and forth frequently (like we do when we're on our phones). Estimates suggest that when you multitask, it takes you 40 per cent longer to finish your original task. This inefficiency slows us down, and it's no wonder that Sherry and the other MIT professors notice that the multitasking students aren't doing as well as the others. Incidentally, it's not just a MIT thing: there's not a single published paper correlating a significant positive relationship between working memory capacity and multitasking![5]

I'm just as lost as everyone else in this matrix of distractions, and as a result, writing this book is taking forever. When I'm working on a tricky sentence that just won't write itself or a passage that is especially difficult, I find myself turning to my phone as a 'break'. Sometimes, an hour passes before I return to writing. Take this chapter, for instance. I started writing when I remembered that I have to look up puppy training techniques (we just got a new puppy). I spent the next half hour watching puppy training videos on YouTube and all that green grass reminded me that I need to book our family vacation. This hyperactive clicking on hyperlinks is highly addictive. In the meantime, I received a message that needed a thoughtful response. Before I knew it, an hour had gone by, and I hadn't written a word. My writer friend Kiran suggested that I try FreeWrite, a writing device with the smarts to be disconnected from the Internet. Zadie Smith would probably buy this new-age typewriter. Almost a decade ago, Zadie said that the key to the sustained attention required to create a novel is to work on a computer that isn't online. That was ten years ago—just think of how much 'stickier' the online experience has become in the last decade.

Stronger, Together

Despite my criticisms, I am acutely aware of how much the Internet has helped me in writing this book about the Internet. It has been a critical resource, a dictionary, an inexhaustible thesaurus, an efficient research assistant and an assiduous fact-checker—all in one. (But I didn't use ChatGPT to write the text, I promise!)

The truth is that, despite the cognitive losses inherent in Internet use, we can't afford to be technophobes. Technology is enormously useful, and the advantages of using technology efficiently are difficult to overstate. Technology continues to teach the human brain new skills, and the Internet's inexhaustible memory has freed up our mental resources. For example, your phone's GPS will direct you to the music concert saving you the task of reading a map or asking for directions which in turn frees up brain space for you to do something else—maybe think of a tune of your own. Most of us don't remember phone numbers anymore, and so our mental resources are free to be creatively used. The Internet gives us the ability to 'cognitively offload' information that we don't need to remember offhand. That's liberating!

Trouble brews when instead of harnessing tech to our brain, *we hand over the reins to technology* leaving us stranded in the shallows. This doesn't mean we should forsake technology or ask our kids to forsake it (not that they'd listen anyway!) We are not making a mistake by innovating, but we must not lose sight of what is lost while we experiment. The choice between technology and the human brain is a false dichotomy; there's no reason that we can't have both. In fact, what if we could use the power of the naked brain and *supplement* (not replace) it with technology to create something that is more than the sum of its parts?

The sun has not yet set on the human brain especially not iGen brains which are still developing. Our brains are wonderfully malleable (which is what got us into this mess in the first place) but the good news is that plasticity can be used to *work alongside technology instead of being replaced by it*. Especially in the age of AI, it is critical that we create this sort of bilingual brain, capable of both retaining its raw processing power and harnessing technology. In this human–machine hybrid which ChatGPT and other AI applications can be, experts will be able to fill in the gaps in the AI's capability, even as the AI becomes more helpful to the expert.[6] There is reason for caution, of course, but there is also reason for excitement. Each of us has a place deep within from which desire pulsates, inspiration flows and imagination soars. It's what makes humans human. Keeping track of what is uniquely human while simultaneously harnessing the enormous capacities of technology—now that's worth the multitasking!

Minimize the Multitask: Pausing the Digital Ping-Pong

Imagine if someone woke you up tomorrow morning and before your feet could hit the floor, immediately placed a ping-pong racket in your hands insisting that you start playing immediately. You have to play from the minute you open your eyes, through your ride to work, in the office, when you caught up with friends for dinner and on the way back home. You have to keep playing even when you finally reached home, exhausted. It doesn't matter if you are eating, working, in the bathroom or watching your kid's piano recital, you have to keep playing ping-pong. Ping. Pong. Ping. Pong. All day long. And when you finally lay down to sleep, you are nudged awake and asked if you really want to sleep. Wouldn't you rather play a little more ping-pong instead? Now, it doesn't matter how hard you've been hitting the gym, your body would break down if this kind of ping-pong was your daily physical regimen. Apply this analogy to your mind because you know your phone is the first thing you reached for this morning. And then it forced you to play ping-pong all day long. We're trying to live at a pace determined by machines and so, is it any surprise that we're all living in a state of near-constant breakdowns?

It's not easy but if you're motivated, here are a few ways to pause the game:

1) Put the Racket Away

Remember to stop and put the racket (your phone) down. Actually, physically put it down. Put it somewhere out of sight, preferably in a desk drawer. Call for a timeout. Drink some water. Give yourself time to breathe, rest and recover. Research insists that digital detoxes are essential if we want to retain optimal cognitive functions including our ability to recall information. Many of us, across the age spectrum, now have 'senior moments', when we just can't seem to remember details. Try not to force it when trying to remember something; that's like revving your car engine without any gas in the tank—it'll never get you anywhere. Refuel yourself by taking a break instead. Simply put, take a break from your smartphone if you want to retain your smarts.

2) Learn from the Dutch

Our impatience is now painfully obvious. 'Talk fast', 'what's the net-net?', 'just give me the bottomline', we direct others. Deadlines are 'the sooner, the better', deliveries need to be instant and if a webpage takes more than a few seconds to open, then it's quickly abandoned. 'Lean in', 'hustle harder', the world yells. With a laptop in one hand, a tablet in another and a phone crammed under our ear, we attempt to do just that. So, when you're advised to put your phone away, you might wonder what to do instead. *Do nothing*, says 'niksen', a Dutch practice that is gaining popularity among psychologists worldwide. Do absolutely nothing. Unplug the Bluetooth headset, set aside the phone and enjoy the pause. Stare out of a window. Lie awake in bed. Watch the grass grow. In a world where being busy has become a status symbol, doing nothing or being purposefully idle seems bizarre. But as one of the happiest nations in the world (and the inventors of the delicious stroopwaffle!), we should trust the Dutch on a thing or two.

Daydreaming—an inevitable effect of idleness—literally makes us more creative, better at problem-solving and better at coming up with creative ideas.[7] Every artist will agree on this: creativity is usually born out of moments of nothingness. It's why you often have your best ideas when you're taking a long shower or lazily stirring a pot. Those tasks help you get out of your head and see things clearly. For too long, we've assumed that being busy is a marker of success when in fact endless busyness could actually hinder progress. So, the next time your child asks you what you're doing, own your idleness and reply proudly, 'I'm doing nothing.' It isn't laziness, it might be the most important skill they'll ever learn.

3) Minimize the Multitask

You aren't built for multitasking. Nobody really is. In fact, every time you try to focus on more than one thing at a time, it is virtually guaranteed that your performance will suffer. The suffering could be trivial, like missing the plotline of a movie or scoring a few marks lower on an exam. It could also be disastrous, which is what happens during most texting and driving accidents. Technology is purposefully designed to be massively disruptive but our brains weren't designed to constantly juggle balls like circus performers. Having three tabs open while writing a paper and checking the news is not what we were made to do. Don't force your brain to multitask. It's like asking a fish to climb a tree.

Two thousand years ago, the Roman philosopher Seneca said, 'To be everywhere is to be nowhere.' There were no smartphones in ancient Rome, but some adages just age well. With that said, you and I don't need an ancient philosopher to tell us what we learned as children: you can't rub your belly and scratch your head at the same time. Go on, try it.

3) Offload, Selectively!

First, there was the reversal of the Flynn effect (we're all turning doltish) and now experts point to the 'Google effect', which is the tendency to forget information that can easily be found online. It's so easy to rely on Google's infinite memory that we're inadvertently diminishing our capacity to remember information. My personal amnesia has become painfully obvious after discovering the Google Thesaurus feature. Now, when I'm looking for an alternative word to describe something, the options float onto the page, I don't even need to search for them. A few weeks into taking this shortcut, I realize I am forgetting where my vocabulary used to live.

To be fair, it's totally fine to offload some things like most phone numbers for instance. You also don't need to remember that you are ten times more likely to be bitten by a New Yorker than a shark.* But in a world where we can hand over our entire brains to technology, *we must intentionally decide how much we want to offload*. For example, at a museum, you are more likely to remember a painting if you actually look at it rather than photograph it. Take the time to experience the things that really matter—things of beauty, works of art, a full moon—rather than just quickly offloading them onto your phone to post online. Some things belong in your brain's cognitive bank and not in your phone's data storage.

4) Find Your Flow

Last night, I was at my daughter's violin recital. Sharply exhaling before entering the auditorium, I readied myself for the sound of nails on a chalkboard. As every parent with a child learning a string instrument knows, the early days can be auditorily challenging. But before the onslaught could begin, the students' violin teacher, Ms Eva, performed a piece for the audience. Eva was likely trying to show us the light at the end of a rather screechy tunnel by demonstrating what a violin can really sound like. When she placed her bow on the instrument, every parent in the audience sat back, transfixed. Eva, an older woman in black slacks with her hair in a low bun, was completely lost in the music of her strings. She was *in the flow*. The psychologist who coined the term 'flow' in the 1960s describes it like this: 'The ego falls away.

---

* I would tell you to Google and confirm that fun fact, but I'm afraid that you'll end up in an endless vortex of New Yorker biting videos and stop reading this book. It's true; just take my word for it.

Time flies. Every action, movement, and thought follows inevitably from the previous one. Your whole being is involved, and you're using your skills to the utmost.'[8] And as Eva played that violin, we flowed with her. It was that rarest of moments when not one person in the audience stirred to check their phone. She made our hearts sing and I wondered how many years of dedication it had taken for her to arrive at this place of wonder. How many years did Eva stay focused on this obscure, high-octave instrument, completely lost to the rest of the world? Watching her play reminded me that it is only when we lose ourselves in the flow that we can truly find ourselves.

Technology has given us a cognitive gift by freeing up some of our mental capacity. To use this newly liberated mental space just to doomscroll through cat videos would be such a waste. Instead, what if we could use it intentionally to build real expertise and go deep into something that really matters? To let the ego fall away, to allow time to fly, to achieve a zen-like state where every movement follows seamlessly from the previous one. It's true that most of us won't end up being concert violinists but I'm realizing that you can achieve flow even while doing the dishes.

CHAPTER SIX

ALL'S NOT LOST: EXPLORING THE BLUE SKIES OF BEING ONLINE

Move Over Ma'am, YouTube is Here

During the horror movie that was April 2020, my friend Sherina wrote on our WhatsApp group chat: 'If I wanted to be a teacher, then dammit, *I would have been a teacher*. I swear all three of my kids have the attention span of gnats. I can't handle this. It's too much!' Several parents in our little neighbourhood group chat sympathized. Crying face emojis ensued. Big bunches of 'hang in there' and 'we're in this together' followed. Emojis be damned; I felt like shedding real tears. Covid had arrived, schools were closed, and everyone was online all the time. Our schools are riddled with pedagogical and infrastructural troubles, but frankly, they seemed like Utopia compared to the haphazard confusion of those early virtual classes. Despite every teacher's best effort, cameras and Internet connections seemed to turn off at will, and the digital divide was on full display as students taught their teachers (and parents!) how to enable the Zoom waiting room, upload assignments on SeeSaw and decode the enduring mystery that is MS Teams. 'Now we know what

Z stands for in Gen Z. It's Zoom!' someone laughed. And sure enough, the common joke among college students became that they attend Zoom University with many of them wearing Zoom University T-shirts to belabour their point. It was a miserable time.

As parents, we can usually find *someone* to blame for any miserable affair concerning our kids. Perhaps one is dealing with a distracted kid who has 'lost focus' and refuses to 'live up to potential' (standard utterances at every PTA meeting), or perhaps the kid has been saddled with an unenthusiastic teacher who is better suited to watching paint dry. But Covid robbed parents of the ability to point fingers at either our children or their teachers. The pandemic was too much, too soon and (sadly) that meant that there was nobody to blame. Until everybody on earth was forced online, teachers in traditional schools had never learned to teach digitally. 'Sure, we all plan our courses but how does one lesson plan for Armageddon?' asked my friend Diksha, a primary school teacher for over fifteen years. Diksha was right: Armageddon was here. Since I couldn't point fingers, I clenched my hands into stressed fists and looked at the debris that was swallowing my house. Test papers were strewn everywhere, essay assignments crowded the dining table, and those physics equations made me want to hurl. A closer look at Zoya's homework assignments revealed that things really had crossed over to nightmare territory: the math had alphabets. Shudder. If I was expected to teach this, then my children would remain unlettered forever.

Enter the digital knight in shining armour: YouTube.

Within minutes of searching online, I found detailed videos on every topic being taught in the school curriculum. *If the triangle in question is not a right-angled triangle, then should one use the sine rule or the cosine rule?* YouTube shows me a college professor ready to demystify trigonometry (clearly his nightmares are different from mine). *What happens when light energy bends as it passes from one type of substance to another?* A video with a million views pops up as a teenage tutor performs experiments to demonstrate this bendy science. *Need to understand the Battle of Panipat in a way that doesn't rival swallowing half a packet of sleeping pills?* Watch an animated video that brings the Mughals, Lodis and their countless horses to life. My droning school history teacher successfully put *herself* to sleep on multiple occasions (true story), but sitting with my children to watch Panipat unfold felt like I was watching a *Game of Thrones* season finale. One of the good finales, in fact.

There was a universe of learning available online and much of it was more informative and interesting than Zoom classes with haunted cameras that turned on and off at will. As the pandemic wore on, this universe seemed to infinitely expand, absorbing unprecedented levels of investment and innovation. In turn, our family absorbed some of this content until everyone's universe expanded including my own. Astoundingly, trigonometry stopped inducing nightmares! Clearly, Covid wasn't the only paradigm shift in town.

Nearly 580 million Indians are aged between five and twenty-four with half of that age group currently enrolled in school. This means that about 36 per cent of our country's population is young and learning. That's a staggering number of Indians vying for the same schools, the same colleges, and often the same courses in the same colleges. To be fair, this hyper-competitiveness isn't necessarily new. Growing up in Delhi in the 1990s, it wasn't unusual to see a student who scored 95 per cent bury their face in their hands in shame. 'Only 95 per cent! I've missed the Eco Honours cut-off. I've done so badly,' went the lament as the rest of us scored full marks in eyerolls. But even though cut-throat competition and impossible cut-offs are old news, what's new is an increasing number of students moving online to survive these hyper-competitive times. This is a huge market for the education sector to leverage, and it's no wonder that India is one of the world's biggest markets for online education.

Better than Brick and Mortar?

Over the years, I have walked in villages and small towns all over the country and found school buildings in the most remote corners. With passing decades, India has built plenty of schools, but the trouble is that we haven't staffed them. An acute shortage of teachers has historically plagued the Indian education system, a woe confirmed by every school principal in India. And in ostensible defiance of market economics, even though teachers are in short supply, those that do teach are grossly underpaid. It's no surprise that many qualified professionals prefer to take on corporate jobs with lucrative pay packages than settle for pennies as teachers. Even those who are passionate about teaching often think of it as a retirement plan, something that can only be done after they've secured the mortgage. This shortage of teachers is set to get worse in brick-and-mortar schools.

After the initial Armageddon days of Covid, many teachers got the hang of teaching online and have since chosen to leave traditional brick-and-mortar schools to join EdTech companies. With enormous upticks in both pay and flexibility, the benefits of this migration are clear. Above-average salaries offered by EdTech firms range from Rs 25 lakh to Rs 2 crore annually along with stock options and flexible work schedules. It's a winning combination which explains why EdTech platforms are flooded with applications. Apart from the pay and flexibility, the sprawling fingers of technology ensure that these teachers can reach students they could never have accessed earlier. Take the case of Sudarshan Gurjar, an erstwhile private tutor based out of Indore, Madhya Pradesh. He joined Unacademy—a multibillion-dollar unicorn—in 2018 and now helps students prepare for their civil service examinations. 'There is more connect. From 100 students during my physical coaching days, I have three lakh followers today,' says Gurjar. Even the best teacher in the world can't reach those numbers without going online.

But is online learning as effective as face-to-face education? It's a question that every parent will ponder at some point and one that can only be answered definitively with the passage of time. However, recent surveys reveal that online instruction appears to be especially effective in large introductory classes with 100 or more students, as those students can use chats and virtual feedback to raise questions they can't ask in large, impersonal lecture halls.[1] I spoke with several students preparing for the dreaded Joint Entrance Examination (JEE) exam, widely regarded as one of the most difficult undergraduate examinations in the world. The preparation is intense, often life-consuming and for many of them, almost entirely online. 'Many of my [online] courses are taught by real-life engineers. I like learning from them because they have a real feel for the subject; their examples and explanations are different,' says Kaushish, who appeared for the exam in 2023. Kaushish is onto something; it is often easier to learn from an expert who has 'been there, done that' than from a teacher who has been teaching the subject for decades but has practised it for zero. 'Imagine a world where learners are taught science by scientists, the arts by philosophers and artists, and languages by native linguists and not generalist educators,' says Sanjay Viswanathan, who leads a hybrid learning platform, Ed4All.[2] I can only think back to my physics teachers who often made us memorize science experiments instead of doing them. But today, a membership to Masterclass.com means Gordon Ramsay will teach me cooking, Indra Nooyi will talk to me about leadership and John Legend will help me with songwriting. And if I want to work on my backhand in my spare time, well then, Serena Williams is ready to coach me through it.

Many studies indicate that India will soon be the online learning capital of the world with several EdTech companies now in the billionaire club and digital pedagogy undergoing a technological alchemy. In schools and colleges where teachers don't show up students are switching to YouTube channels that 'cover' their syllabus.[3] While offline classes have attempted to make learning more interesting, the truth is that online learning offers what the offline medium never could: it appeals to iGen's addiction to the visual. Companies are using games, music and videos to make learning more interesting and interactive. And students are responding to this innovation: nearly 70 per cent of students stated that gamified courses are more motivating than traditional ones. Covid may have retreated but administrators around the world unanimously agree that college and university students will now be online for at least part of their educations.[4]

All of this made sense to me when I tuned in to a recent cricket match. Nothing in India speaks louder than a cricket bat, and when our men in blue entered the *maidan*, their shirts were no longer emblazoned with logos of credit card companies or cement manufacturers. The national team was sponsored by Byju's, an EdTech unicorn with a multibillion-dollar valuation.

Closing the Gap (Finally!)

Not all education is equal and it's likely that your domestic help's child who attends the village school is two grades behind your child, even if both kids were born in the same year. This gap between 'rich schools' and 'poor schools' in India is so entrenched that it was long considered unbridgeable. Until EdTech disrupted the space. With private players like Esper collaborating with Teach for India to ship pre-loaded tablets directly to students' doorsteps, we finally have the opportunity to level the playing field. The government also sees the opportunity—and necessity—to reach out to these children and has launched several initiatives to bring rural education in India up to par with global best practices in online education. Teaching is often cheaper if done through a screen and technology might finally help us achieve 'Education for All', a dream that has eluded us so far.

And just like *how* things are taught is being revolutionized, *what* is being taught is going through a revolution too. Digital skill creators teach diverse practical skills such as woodworking, glassblowing and how to use MS office, as well as soft skills such as fluency in spoken English and speaking with a polished accent. Millions of people learn millions of things on YouTube with 72 per cent of respondents in India saying they were actively learning digital skills to prepare for the future of work. I was on a flight last week and sat next to a middle-aged teacher who said she was now learning advanced French. *'Tres bon!'* I thought since I've been interested in brushing up my French too. I asked her where she went for her classes. 'YouTube,' she replied without skipping a beat. My friend Pranav tells me that he watches YouTube videos before transactions. 'I've learned so much from these videos from negotiation 101 to business strategy. You've got the real folks telling you what's worked for them in their boardrooms. It's better than any MBA!' Millions of Indians search YouTube for ideas on to how to achieve rocket-ship growth in their lives with videos such as 'How to Make Rs 1 crore in three years' and 'How to Become a Billionaire in 2023' mopping up millions of views. And wouldn't you know it, YouTube videos on 'How to Make Money from YouTube' are also incredibly popular.

But it's not just YouTube entrepreneurs; we are living in an unprecedented time in world history in which the opinions of presidents, the distilled knowledge of Nobel Laureates and the expertise of Olympians are only a click away. Every one of us, everywhere, is within arm's reach of information, opinions and learnings about everything, old and new. Knowledge is no longer static words in dusty books but rather a living entity that can be updated with new information in real-time. When Pluto is demoted to a dwarf planet, the Internet instantly updates itself even though the school science book continues to insist on nine full-sized planets. Instead of being stuck with the uncooperative kid next on the roll call, our children can use technology to connect with others who share their goals. Many students in my daughter's science class have chosen to collaborate with lab partners on another continent. From Christina Aguilera helping you improve your stage presence to a French native demonstrating how to correctly pronounce *pain au chocolate*, there are endless options to enhance our lives backed by the collective intelligence of an infinite network.

Here Comes the Hotstepper—AI!

To be sure, the boundaries of this intelligent network are being pushed every day. Which of us hasn't marvelled at ChatGPT, the powerful AI tool that can make quick work of a thorny math problem or write a doctoral thesis in seconds. From writing computer code to Shakespearean essays—there seems to be nothing that ChatGPT can't do! My friend, Sav, a tech enthusiast has taken to conversing with ChatGPT on a dizzying array of topics. I asked the man what he talks about to the machine. 'Everything,' he replied, 'from God to air pollution.' Here are some of their recent conversation starters:

1. What is the meaning of life?
2. Does God exist?
3. Explain what a black hole is in simple terms.
4. Write 1000 words about the video game Super Mario brothers.
5. What are great activities for parents to do with their kids aged under ten and over four over the weekend?
6. Is ChatGPT self-aware?
7. If I were to start a fashion e-commerce site to discover and shop matching fashion, what key features would I include?
8. If I was to start a business at the intersection of medical testing, fitness and nutrition, what key features would I need?
9. Write 1000 words on the Indus Valley Civilization.
10. What are the best Chinese restaurants on the Palm Jumeirah in Dubai?
11. What is the meaning of the Bhagvad Gita?
12. How do siblings in their forties have a great relationship for the rest of their lives when they live in different parts of the world?
13. Explain APIs in a language that non-technical people would understand.
14. How do I become better at sight reading on the piano?
15. How do I deal with the reality that my parents are ageing and that their health is declining when I know that no one is going to last forever?

16. How would a new coffee startup in India differentiate from the existing major chains?
17. What safety precautions can I take to protect myself from Mumbai's terrible air pollution?
18. What are the differences between psychodynamic and CBT therapy?
19. What are the qualities of a best friend?
20. I want to become a National Geographic photographer. How do I become one?

The response to each question is clear, succinct and often introspective. It seems like the bot is alive and sentient. It feels like it's actually thinking. Inspired by Sav, I start to chat with ChatGPT and it isn't long before the bot begins to feel like a friend. A funny, wise and infinitely intelligent friend. Want your friend to be wiser? Funnier? Smarter? ChatGPT will comply with all requests in seconds. But it's not just existential conversations or structured business plans, ChatGPT has upended the most fundamental part of the human experience—teaching and learning. The quality of its responses on virtually any topic is outperforming most students and given that it can grade assignments, it's no wonder that many teachers are feeling threatened too! Daniel Herman has been teaching English for twelve years and is dazzled by the quality of ChatGPT's writing. 'If you're looking for historical analogues, [ChatGPT] would be like the printing press, the steam drill, and the light bulb having a baby, and that baby having access to the entire corpus of human knowledge and understanding,' says Herman.[5] In similar recognition of the chatbot's talent, the International Baccalaureate (IB) board announced that ChatGPT will now be allowed in IB essays.[6]

But not everyone has been as cool as the IB board—many are feeling threatened by the new baby on the academic block. Thousands of teachers are redesigning courses, school administrators are trying to block ChatGPT and companies are trying desperately to develop anti-plagiarism tools. But as the world scrambles, the kids are enjoying this nifty gift that can demolish every exam and assignment. 'ChatGPT just finished writing all my final papers. I'm going dancing! Enjoy studying you guys!' says a breezy young woman on Tiktok. And just in case you're worried that you'll get caught cheating, another TikToker @carterpcs, suggests this breakthrough solution to his four million followers: 'First you go to CactusAI to have the essay written, then you find an essay or email that you actually wrote, and then you finally go to ChatGPT and tell it to rewrite the CactusAI message in the style of your writing.' And boom, there it is! A brand-new essay of any length, ready in minutes and so perfectly customized to your style of writing that your professor can't possibly quibble.

As staggering as it already is, AI is just getting started. ChatGPT is remarkable not only for what it can do today but because it is a harbinger of what is coming tomorrow.[*] The technology is in its toddler stage and who knows what it will grow into. These are uncertain times and every day that goes by, AI performs a new task that shocks the world. The next decades will see AI advancements that are impossible to predict and police. But instead of getting into an endless game of cat and mouse with AI, teachers

---

[*] We'd also best remember that AI is improving at a remarkable pace while human intelligence really isn't.

worldwide are better off incorporating this technology into classrooms. Our kids are going to graduate into a world filled with ChatGPT's descendants and they will need to know how to deploy these tools wisely and safely.

What we can do as parents? Even though the pace of this technology is breathtaking, we would do well to pause and inhale. Education may have been upended but learning hasn't become outdated. In fact, the age-old lessons might be more important today than ever before. What it takes to truly collaborate, how to maintain sustained focus rather than bouncing from app to app, listening to diverse opinions instead of falling into social media's echo chambers. None of these lessons can be taught by AI, no matter how advanced. For this, we'll always need our teachers.

Lightning in a Bottle:
Social Media Careers

Everyone became a virologist during Covid, swapping terms like vaccine efficacy, comorbidity and dysgeusia as though we were medical school toppers. 'I know what we should do to flatten the curve,' I found myself saying through a mouthful of bread while fattening my own curves. Given that any phone can become a megaphone, our feeds quickly flooded over with 'expert' advice from epidemiologists without degrees and economists who couldn't tell a bell from a bar.

As we pass the megaphone around, each of us can become a celebrity for a day. Gone are the iconic figures who radiated mystique, remained untouchable and lived light-years away. They shone; they were larger than life, and perhaps, it's no wonder that we called them 'stars'. Today's stars don't shine in mysterious, faraway galaxies. Social media allows even the most ordinary among us to be part of the constellation. 'If there is anything I've learned about kids today, and I'm not saying that this is good or bad, it's that they all want to be a star,' says Hollywood producer Dan Schneider. And, in India, you no longer have to be the Badshah of Bollywood or the God of Cricket to be a star—technology makes space for us all.

Of course, not everyone deserves the megaphone, and my mother seems to have a direct hotline to every undeserving candidate. A few weeks ago, she phoned me in state of a panic. 'Just check your WhatsApp. I've sent you the message,' she said as though she was a CIA agent in possession of a top-secret document. Her hyperventilation collided with my sighs as I read the message written in all caps: 'IMPORTANT MESSAGE FROM DELHI POLICE . . . 4 NEXT FEW DAYS DONT CONSUME ANY PRODUCT FROM PEPSI, TROPICANA JUICE SLICE, 7UP, COCA COLA, ETC. AS A WORKER FROM D COMPANY HAS ADDED HIS BLOOD CONTAMINATED WITH AIDS. Plz Forward this message to every 1 u care 4.' I slowly popped open a can of Pepsi while she was still on the phone. And yes, I made sure my mom heard my pop.

But just like tech gives a microphone to mischief-makers, it also gives a megaphone to real talent that otherwise might have waited in the wings. Regardless of whether you sided with KJo or Kangana in the 'Great Battle of Nepotism' you'll likely agree on one thing: the gates to the entertainment industry, like every other trade, are closely guarded. Of course, there are exceptions—megastars like Amitabh Bachchan and Shahrukh Khan among them—but these largely prove the pervasive rule. The Internet, and particularly social media, has blown these guarded gates wide open. Anisha Dixit, a popular YouTuber, started making videos after failing to make it in Bollywood. Her most popular video has over twelve million views. 'I love the fact that I can reach this kind of audience without having to audition,' she says.[7]

Bhuvan Bam, one of India's most popular YouTubers, is an industry 'outsider'. He popped on to his Instagram to say that he'll drop his new music video a day earlier if he receives 25,000 comments in three hours. My jaw stayed on the floor as his account racked up 1,00,000 comments in under sixty minutes! That's star power that would make coiffed heads turn at any Bollywood party. And speaking of parties, everyone gets an invite—age no bar! I am hanging out on @Mr_and_Mrs_Verma, an account run by two senior citizens. I watch as Mr and Mrs Verma, both in their seventies, slide and groove to the latest Insta reel trend as Rasheeda's *Marry Me* plays in the background . . .

> *Boy you know you wanna put a ring on my finger, finger, finger*
> *Put it on him make him wanna marry me (Yeah)*
> *Put it on him make him wanna marry me (Yeah)*
> *Put it on him make him wanna marry me (Yeah)*
> *Put it on him, make him- pu- pu- put it on him, make him . . .*

Aside from grooving to Rasheeda, Mr and Mrs Verma can also be seen endorsing pain relief patches for ageing joints, serenading each other around their grandchildren and cleaning their Nike high-tops (Mr Verma is a sneakerhead). They are part of a growing number of 'granfluencers' in India, who are challenging the stereotype of the doddering *dada-dadi*. A new career at seventy? They're here for it. In other corners of the Internet, artists are being discovered after posting their music on SoundCloud while authors have become literary sensations after publishing short novels on their cell phones. Many of these success stories are being propelled by the collective power of half a billion Indians who watch YouTube on their phones—in village squares and town centres, hotels and homes, factories and farms, cars and buses. With such a large audience, it's clear that a single post on *literally anything*—photography, smoothies, digital art or cats—can change your life. Social media is like lightning in a bottle and with every post, you can come closer to making thunder.

Breakdowns Are Occupational Hazards

Social media is the world's most crowded marketplace and regardless of whether you're making a YouTube video or an Insta Reel, it takes exceptional grit to consistently capture the planet's attention. As frivolous as these posts may seem, each piece of content takes serious work. Many digital creators are production houses unto themselves as they are often the writer, editor, director and producer of their show. *They are both the star and the spot boy*. And unlike TV shows that have seasons that allow artists to catch their breath, YouTube never turns off. In fact, the platform's algorithm rewards creators who post new content round the clock and rachet up viewer engagement through likes and subscriptions. Running at breakneck speed on the YouTube treadmill, amidst the noise of new competition pouring in every day, creators must constantly keep posting or risk being thrown off the machine. '[YouTube] kind of is a machine,' says Lilly Singh who has almost fifteen million subscribers on the platform. 'It makes creators believe that we have to pump out content consistently, even at the cost of our lives, our mental health and our happiness. Because if you don't, then you'll become "irrelevant".'[8] Rohan Joshi, who has been posting comedic content for over a decade, puts it more bluntly, 'You find yourself putting things out there just because the algo needs feeding. Or because you miss likes and engagement. What a backward-ass way to create, tilling the recesses of your mind just to feed a monster that will never ever be full or nourished. A monster that is designed to forget you the second you stop feeding it.'[9] A short reel that takes a minute to watch often represents days of work, and many creators report working 100-hour workweeks just to feed YouTube. Essentially, neither the star nor the spot boy ever gets a break.

Since the platform doesn't allow you to pause, many creators are forcing themselves to take a break before they burn out. In a YouTube video titled *Burnt Out at 19*, Elle Mills, a massively popular YouTube creator, said she was clocking out of the platform. She isn't alone. 'I am mentally, physically, emotionally and spiritually exhausted,' said Lilly, who has also taken a break from YouTube. Rohan posted that he's no longer energized by the relentless 'manufacturing or inventing thoughts just to feed the algorithm' and that going forward he will be posting much less. His comment section filled with popular Indian content creators echoing similar sentiments. Clearly, many creators are feeling the burn, and unsurprisingly, nearly half of surveyed influencers[10] felt their job as an influencer had negatively impacted their mental health. That's a serious occupational hazard.

But hazardous or not, content creators don't usually leave their platforms permanently. 'Breaks' are often just that: interludes to refuel before returning to recreate the magic. According to CreatorIQ, roughly half of YouTube creators who have quit (or said they were going to quit) resumed making videos after taking a break. 'To be clear, this isn't some "goodbye Instagram" post,' writes Rohan Joshi in his 'taking a break' post. 'That's not how addiction works.'[11]

Show Me the Money

But it's not just addiction to likes. In today's attention economy, capturing eyeballs often translates into real cash. Kim Kardashian one of the highest-paid celebrities of our time, earns more money from Instagram than from an entire season of her superhit TV series. Kim is the perfect example of an Internet celebrity whose core product is herself. And at close to a million dollars per post, she is a massively profitable core product. Her product endorsement could be something as simple as a photograph of a smoothie placed between photos of her children and a fabulous yacht. This is exactly the kind of subversive hook that advertisers love because it creates an emotional bond that is unmatched by traditional advertising. Social media marketing works at so many subliminal levels that as I follow her posts on Instagram, a part of me begins to believe that I am friends with Kim.

I find it hard to remember that my access to Kim does not establish a symmetrical friendship based on trust; instead, it is usually intended to capture more of [my] one-sided devotion, for commercial ends.[12] I lose sight of this asymmetry as our 'friendship' deepens and I spend more time on her account, seeing more of her posts. *We're getting to know each other better*; I think as I heart her latest post and she pockets another million dollars. In India, Kim would go head-to-head with Virat Kohli who currently has the country's largest Instagram following. At over 250 million followers, he charges just under Rs 9 crore for a single Instagram post.[13]

But you don't need to have Kohli or Kardashian-sized mega followings to generate decent revenue on social media. Lickd's Social Salary calculator estimates that content creators with roughly 5000 followers can earn an average of $350 for a post. This number jumps exponentially as followers increase and those with more than 1,00,000 followers can expect to make over $4000 per post. Popular Instagrammer Kritika Khurana @BohoGirl estimates that (non-Bollywood and non-cricket) Instagrammers in India charge between Rs 10,000 and Rs 90,000 per static post, with videos going up to Rs 3 lakh each.[14] Your earnings also depend on the kind of advertising that can be placed alongside your content, she explains.

In 2021, *Forbes* magazine exclaimed that twenty-three-year-old Jimmy Donaldson, aka MrBeast, was the top-earning YouTuber worldwide with earnings of approximately $54 million.[*] That's no small change and

---

[*] For more context on MrBeast's outsized influence on iGen, flip back to this book's Introduction.

YouTube has its way of rewarding content and adding up the dollars. A channel's revenue is determined through complex metrics that include measuring the number of active viewers, the number of subscribers as well as audience engagement (through likes and comments). And to continue to grow revenue sources for influencers, social media platforms are constantly adding tools such as Badges on Instagram and Stars on Facebook, which can be directly monetized.

Snapchat has over 249 million daily users, and recently launched a feature called Spotlight to drive more content production. Snapchatter Sarati made it to *Forbes* for her income through Snapchat alone, and more than 2000 Snapchatters have earned from a pool of $42 million, with top performer Cam Casey earning over a cool $3 million.

The money is rolling in because virtually every company with a product to sell is moving to shoppable media: an interactive buying experience that sits at the intersection of content and commerce. Content and buying experiences are converging, and the relationship is bidirectional. People can now consume content where they shop and shop where they consume content. Purchasing products directly on social media, in gaming environments and through streaming video services is already commonplace. Last year alone, goods worth over an estimated $500 billion were sold via livestream or short video platforms in China.[15] You showcase your product— say a brand of homemade chocolate—on livestream with viewers typing in their orders and their preferred flavour, hazelnut or caramel, all while you unwrap the bar online.

Gaming platforms already host millions of users in immersive environments, where players can buy virtual clothing and gestures to personalize their avatars, brands can advertise and sell virtual goods, and media franchises can create in-game experiences based on their intellectual property (IP). Top artists perform larger-than-life concerts reaching millions of fans around the world most of whom are watching from their living room couch. Today, the money trail no longer leads to your shopping mall nearest you, it probably leads to the closest device.

Blue Tick for Baby: The World of Family Vlogs

In a world where your device can turn anything into a money spinner, it's tempting to commercialize all of it. Everything—your voice, your words, your cooking skills, your family—can be traded for likes and cash. Culturally, we are a country obsessed with family drama, a trend that the queen of soaps, Ekta Kapoor realized early on. Cashing in on this same fascination with family drama is a torrent of vlogs that are mopping up millions of views as they become some of the Internet's most-watched genres. In fact, family vlogs are so lucrative that some parents may adopt children for views only to return them soon after.[16] Sarah runs the popular @mom.uncharted TikTok account where she calls out many of these vlogs. 'It almost feels like exploiting your children has become a career choice,' she says to her 2,00,000+ followers. 'If you have a baby now, you have a new career opportunity.' But reprehensible adoption practices aside, it's easy to see why family vlogs have taken the Internet by storm. *Want to watch someone's kid have a meltdown in the middle of the mall?* Sure. *Interested in seeing a husband and wife rabidly argue about his parents?* Yes please. *How about sitting back and watching a mother rant about the pressures of raising kids?* Let's go! With family vlogs, it's as though the most interesting people in the world moved into the house next door and then took down all their walls. No walls, no boundaries. Someone bring the popcorn! But despite being wildly entertaining, these vlogs make for problematic content considering that they often commercialize those who cannot reasonably give consent. Yes, we're back to worrying about the kids.

I'm watching a massively popular family vlogger who frequently features his children in his content. In one of the vlogs, his five-year-old daughter has just fallen down when the father grabs the camera to record the incident. The child does eventually receive first aid but the whole saga—including the child's screams—is recorded and uploaded. In another vlog, a visibly afraid young boy is being reprimanded by his parents. The parents proceed to admonish the child all the while recording his reaction as he cowers in a corner, frightened out of his wits. The video does massively well. There are videos with millions of views in which, for instance, a ten-year-old boy is made to feel responsible for his mother's miscarriage. The boy starts crying; his outburst is then recorded, uploaded, watched millions of times and ultimately monetized.

Sometimes it's hard to tell if these reactions are real. In a now-deleted video,[17] a popular family blogger, Jessica, tells her eight-year-old son that his puppy is sick and will likely die. The young boy is obviously upset (his puppy is dying), and Jessica is recording his reaction. She wants to capture this moment for her 5,00,000+ followers.

She coaches her son on his reaction to the news of his dying puppy.

'Come closer,' Jessica tells him. 'Act like you're crying.'

'I *am* crying,' the boy replies. 'Mom, I'm actually seriously crying.'

The mother then proceeds to tell him *how* to cry for the camera. 'Let them see your mouth,' she says. 'Look at the camera.' It's enough to make anyone cry.

The Internet has now been around long enough to have adults who were raised on family channels of all shapes and sizes. Some of them were in utero when their parents started sharing their pregnancy journeys; others had opened their mouths for their first bite when their mothers started posting baby food recipes; and there are millions who have had their first diaper change, their first tantrum and their first bath viewed by strangers across the world. Some of these children—now grown adults—have had the time to process this experience and the impact it continues to have on their lives. Lou, twenty-six, is one of the first adults who is speaking up about the pressures of being raised on a 'mommy vlog'.[18] 'Nothing was sacred,' Lou says. 'There was that constant feeling of "being on", which meant that even in the privacy of our home, you could always expect the camera to be around. Any conversation . . . regardless of how embarrassing or intimate or private it was, could end up on the blog.' Family vlogs around the world are full of intimate moments—meltdowns, breakdowns, embarrassing accidents—and each high-octave moment makes for great viewing. Even as an adult, Lou stays trapped in a downward spiral created by this oversharing of her childhood. 'It was all for the consumption of strangers. Even now, as a twenty-six-year-old . . . I'm still so stressed about how I appear and how it's going to be received by strangers, even when I'm just having a quiet moment with my spouse. I feel obligated to share those moments, and they're not for consumption,' she says, her voice quivering as she speaks. A commenter responds to Lou's video and writes, 'I was raised in a similar situation [being featured on a family vlog] and it's made me intensely private, and I don't have photos of myself or my family up in my home as a result.'

I am speaking to Kaveri, a teenager whose entire life from toddlerhood to the teen years has been posted and monetized by her parents. 'Nothing about my life is ever off limits to the camera,' she says. 'Now I'm at a point where I have to hide my life from my parents because otherwise, I know it'll be posted on TikTok tomorrow morning.' While Kaveri is choosing not to say much, others are sending a very clear message to their parents. One child of influencers started a website called Quit Clicking Kids that combats the monetization of children on social media. Quit Clicking Kids—the name says it all.

I know what Kaveri, Lou and others mean when they speak of an invasion of privacy. During our childhood vacations, it was always my mother who encouraged us to take photographs. It was annoying to pause what we were doing and pose for the camera but today, those sepia albums of our touristy moments—our arms casually slung around one another while posing under Big Ben or getting a Limca outside the Konark temple— are among my most precious possessions. Their limited number only adds to their charm: camera film rolls were expensive and with twenty-four photos on a roll, you had to choose wisely—not every moment needed to be a photograph. When we returned home from vacation, unpacking the suitcases was left to our parents while my sister and I raced to the photoshop in Delhi's Khan Market to get the films developed. I recall the shopkeeper once leeringly handing me the envelope of photo prints. 'London *ghoom aaye?*' he asked. I felt invaded in that moment—this stranger had clearly flipped through our family photographs. And although I felt violated, I realize my indignation pales in comparison to what Lou and others like her have experienced while growing up on family vlogs. For them, every moment is a photograph that the whole planet can view anytime they want, and even the right to feel invaded is off-limits.

To be fair, not every child will be negatively impacted, and many, if not most, family vlogs start out with noble intentions. My friend Shreyasi runs a family vlog with her three adorable sons, all under the age of five. She posts upbeat videos as the boys bake cakes and learn phonics. Each of their angelic faces seems made for the camera, and I can see why they pull in the views. 'The boys love making these videos,' Shreyasi insists. 'Even when I'm not recording, they'll constantly ask, "Mom, where's the camera?" The other day, they were arguing about their toys, and one of the boys turned around and said, "Mom, put our fight on the camera!" They love being on!' When I asked Shreyasi about her goals for the vlog, she said she 'dreams of going viral, of hitting a million views, maybe more'. With faces that beatific, I can imagine those videos going viral one day. But such success comes at a cost when the stars of the show are so young. New followers means thousands of new people to impress, as well as the pressure to now go from viral to mega-viral. They're close to mastering their phonics and soon Shreyasi's kids will learn to read. It won't be long before they encounter their comment section that will range from compliments to the (sadly) inevitable 'u r so ugly, u should kill yourself.'

While family vlogs may seem innocuous, the indelible nature of the Internet means content—especially public content—is a permanent life decision. Digital footprints that they didn't create will follow these children for the rest of their lives which means they will never have a blank page on which to write their own stories. I've watched video after video of kids who were happy to play along with the family vlog when they were younger but stopped wanting to participate as they got older. Children often resent being commoditized after the phase of craving parental validation has passed. And even though the vast majority of family vlogs start off with the simple intention of sharing family moments, growing the channel requires dedicated hustle. This could involve posting nudies of toddlers, forcing reluctant kids to perform for a camera (cry harder for your sick puppy), or creating emotionally charged situations that deliver more views (you caused my miscarriage). By crossing that line, the vlog itself crosses over from a well-intentioned platform that captures family moments to a business that prioritizes views over well-being. Parents become employers, YouTube metes out both reward and punishment and many kids are caught in the crosshairs of these crossovers.

Yet again the law loses the race to technology as currently, there are no rules to protect the earnings of these child influencers. But apart from the money, family vlogs are riddled with questions, both ethical and physiological, that need answering before content is shared online.

How will my child handle the dopamine rush that comes with chasing likes? How does our family get our child's consent before they can even write their name? Is our kid equipped to deal with the stress that comes from an Internet career? As the legendary Tina Fey says, 'You can read a hundred different positive comments on social media, but you'll only remember the one bad one.' Are our children prepared to deal with the savage jungle that is a public comment section? These questions may be inconvenient but they're necessary especially when the star of the show isn't the one who craves the blue tick.

Game On: How Play Can Really Pay

My mother insists that parenting is a never-ending job. 'It's one of those *permanent positions*,' she sighs dramatically, 'with no salary and no retirement age.' She's clearly hinting at something, but I roundly refuse to take the bait. She perseveres. 'The shape of your worries changes,' she continues at the end of a rather long exhale, 'but this is a lifetime job. You never stop being a parent.'

Insinuations aside, I grudgingly see her point; parenting often seems to be about accepting a baseline of permanent, shapeshifting worry. At the nursing stage, it's all about survival. *But is the baby breathing?* wonders every new parent, breathlessly peering into the crib wondering who left them in charge of this helpless creature that mysteriously arrived without an instruction manual. And just as the panic about breathing settles, the primary school years begin with a flurry of firsts: the first uniform, the first timetable, the first broken elbow, the first homework giving way to the first crush and the first fistfight. And before the child enters secondary school, we—now decade-old parents—hyperventilate anew. There's fresh panic in the air: yes, the kids are breathing *but are they achieving?* 'A is for achievement,' we tell them. 'A is for accolades. A is for awards.' 'Bring home the A's!' we yell. Rearing racehorses, we demand that they 'perform well' in school, scheduling multiple parent–teacher meetings to discuss said performance in detail.

'How's my kid doing in class?' we inquire during those meetings. But the question we're really asking is: *How do I ensure that my child comes out on top so that they can get the right job?* Ask any secondary school teacher, most of these conversations are underpinned by a common theme: the kid's eventual performance as a stable, career-holding, card-carrying member of the adult fraternity rather than their inherent interest in the subjects being taught (or not taught) in school. And so, hidden somewhere in the comments on that report card, beneath those gleaming A's, the glimmers of a future doctor, banker or lawyer appear. As our children grow older, we can almost see lawyers' robes replacing school uniforms and we mentally mark a spot on the wall to hang their doctor's degree. We breathe a little easier; the kids are 'on track', we think, (there we go with racehorses again). And conversely, it doesn't strike us that a report card with lower grades could indicate that the kid has alternative skills or is simply disinterested in an outdated schooling system. Instead, an imperfect report card is terrorizing because it pulls away the carpet from underneath our feet. Everything seems unsteady as we imagine our children falling behind in the race of life. *Come on, don't lose the race,* we pant; *be serious, kid. Get to work.*

Games, by association, are antithetical to work. This association runs so deep that the words have acquired opposing connotations, such as 'fun' for the former and 'boring' for the latter. '*Padoge likhoge toh banoge Nawab, kheloge koodoge toh hoge kharab*,' instructed a popular yesteryear Bollywood song. I grew up listening to my grandfather recite this line like an anthem to each of his six grandchildren. *Kheloge koodoge toh hoge kharab*, he'd repeat as we abandoned our maths homework for yet another game of hide and seek. And listening to similar admonishments, slowly, an entire generation learned to stop playing games. Lest we go bad. And now when we spot iGen obsessed with video games, it fills us with terror. *What if they become kharab?* we panic.

The New Battlefield

Much of our anxiety is misplaced and probably even counterproductive. By fretting about traditional careers, we inexorably push our children into a horserace with no finish line. AI is replacing humans at an unprecedented rate in many conventional industries (including writing books!) causing these already overcrowded spaces to burst at the seams. By forcing them into crowded careers that they were never particularly keen on, most children are unlikely to become reputable or happy engineers, doctors or lawyers even if they do land the job. Could it be time to consider alternative careers and perhaps rewrite the whole phrase? *Padoge likhoge toh banoge Nawab, kheloge koodoge toh banoge lajawab* might be a more accurate prediction for these times. Play is the new work, and it's time to level up and say hello to gaming.

Few industries are as fast-paced as gaming. Processors now move at lightning speed, memory space has grown exponentially while smartphones and budget laptops are ubiquitous. Research indicates that the world now has 3.3 billion gamers—close to half the global population! India continues to be one of the world's leading gaming markets with the country's percentage of new paying gamers being the fastest growing in the world. Aditya Sawant aka Dynamo, one of India's top gamers, points out, '*Mobile gamers aapko har jagah mil jayenge. Aapke galli mein bahut sare bache khel rahe honge. Aapke office ke neeche ya aapke office mein hi.*' Aditya knows what he's talking about: his Dynamo Gaming YouTube channel alone has ten million subscribers.

It's impossible to discuss the Indian video game market without talking about *PUBG* or its rebranded post-ban avatar, *Battlegrounds Mobile India*. If you haven't responded to its irresistible call to arms by playing *PUBG*, you've encountered it in the numerous government bans that have turned the game into a real-life battleground. At your office, in your kids' school and around your neighbourhood *galli*, *PUBG* is everywhere. The game has acquired a global following, but its actual premise is quite simple. *PUBG* is a first-person shooter game in which soldiers parachute onto an abandoned island with a singular objective: to be the last man standing. The winner's reward is even simpler—a virtual chicken dinner. 'Winner Winner, Chicken Dinner!' flashes the screen. Everyone from children to the world's most elite athletes is crazy about those four words. Before the *PUBG* ban, the Board of Control for Cricket in India (BCCI) tweeted[19] a photo of the Indian cricket team waiting for a flight. It's not the usual photo that one sees of cricket players looking determined as they stride on to a field; in this shot, not a single player is looking up—they're all busy playing *PUBG*! '*PUBG ne poora scene hee change kar diya*,' says popular gamer CarryMinati. He's right. Keeping iGen away from video games is both impossible and unfair in this new environment; it would deprive them of a critical component of their time, a portal to both work and play.

One of the reasons games are so important to iGen is their unique ability to connect them with others, friends and strangers alike. As players gather to run, jump and shoot, the camaraderie on the screen is palpable. '*PUBG* has made so many friendships, and even so many marriages. Really!' exclaims Shazia Ayub aka Mysterious YT, an avid gamer. I understand what she means. This game is fun to play. It's free. It's easy to download. It's on your cell phone, which means it lives in your pocket; it's designed to be played wherever you are. And because the game is team-based, you are constantly communicating with other players to create a community. As Naman Mathar aka Soul Mortal, one of India's top *PUBG* players says, '. . . the game lets you communicate with each other. There are a hundred people dropping, and you have to survive with your teammate. Your coordination, your strategy, how you kill the other players by yourself, how to loot. This game has everything. You communicate with people you don't know. After talking, you might realize you stay nearby, then you might meet over coffee or anything.'[20] I see Naman's point. I'm at lunch with a friend who has brought her ten-year-old son, Yash along to lunch. Before I can ask if he might feel bored with us,

Yash whips out his phone. Within minutes, he is playing FIFA online with the boy at the next table. The two have never met before but months later, they are still in touch. Online, of course.

Aside from new friends, superstar video game players have super-sized fan followings with many gamers enjoying an almost cult-like celebrity status. Move over Bollywood, CarryMinati is so well-known that he can hardly leave the house anymore. 'He recently went to a shopping mall. A fan tore off his shirt, another punched me, someone else kissed him on the cheek,' says Anirudh Nagpal, CarryMinati's manager. Their fans may not recognize a gamer's face or even know their real name but make no mistake: this is celebrityhood like you've never seen before. During one of Dynamo's *PUBG* livestreams, I get a front-row seat to the fanfare. This is what happens: Dynamo is on the battlefield when an unknown soldier starts running straight towards him. Dynamo's teammate prepares to shoot the solider down when Dynamo yells, '*Mat maar. Mat maar.* He's come to say hi.' What follows is what might have happened if a cricket fan were to bump into Tendulkar at the local coffee shop. The unknown soldier falls to his knees and sobs uncontrollably. 'I never imagined that I'd be standing in front of you,' he cries, and I can hear his voice trembling through my headset. The sobs continue for a while until Dynamo graciously moves forward and lifts the fan up. 'Don't cry, don't cry,' says Dynamo as the soldier continues to heave uncontrollably. Shoulder to shoulder, they then enter battle together, the fan's voice still trembling.

It took me a while to wrap my head around this video. For that fan, Dynamo's avatar's heroic actions were as real as the deliveryman ringing the doorbell or his mother urging him to study. You see, iGen does not differentiate between IRL and avatars the way we might. On his part, Dynamo says the attention is great but admits that things are starting to feel strange. 'I find it weird because I can never see their face. I can only hear their voice. This virtual reality is changing into a reality.'

Gamers may make it appear easy, but this kind of recognition is hard-won. Serious gamers, like many other online professionals, work long hours every day. They are continuously practising their game, often training six or seven days a week. They must maintain their diet, follow dedicated physical activity routines and remain drug-free to participate in international gaming competitions. Then there are gaming boot camps, where gamers gather under one roof while practising around the clock. '*Unka khaana-peena, sona-uthna sab ek saath hota hai,*' says a gamer. Gaming is no child's play.

Serious gaming requires hundreds of hours of practice and often comes at the cost of other pursuits which may well include academics. Unsurprisingly, many top *PUBG* players suggested that the real battle was being fought at home. Frustrated parents insisted on academic performance while kids saw their future on an online battlefield. The outcome is often protracted, emotional confrontations between physics books and *PUBG* battlefields. For Rohan Ledwani, aka HydraFlick, choosing gaming over academics is an obvious choice. He believes that gaming teaches lessons that school does not: '*Agar tum school mein fail hote ho, toh tum par yeh "failed" ka tag aa jata hai*. In gaming, you learn to retry, to do something again and again, *jab tak tum usme perfect nahin ban jaate. Jo school mein nahi sikhaya jaata, par gaming mein hai,*' he says with conviction. Perhaps the most disarmingly honest answer about the trade-off between gaming and studying comes from Rony Dasgupta, aka RawKnee, a gamer with over four million YouTube subscribers. '*Padtha kaun hai?*' he asks imperiously. '*Woh kya tha . . . Pytho . . . Pytho . . . kya tha . . .? Haan, pythagoras! Ghanta Pythagoras,*' he exclaims. '*Ghanta Pythagoras,*' exclaim iGen gamers as parent–teacher councils quiver in disbelief!

SoulMortal says gaming took over his life in 2015: '*Raat raat mein khelte the, din mein khelte the, poora time, college mein, bahar.*' His parents pleaded with him to focus on college instead, but everything changed when one of his *PUBG* YouTube videos went viral, giving him the sign he needed to double down on gaming. Today, he feels he owes *PUBG* everything. '*Agar PUBG nahi hota toh shayad mein nahi hota,*' says SoulMortal. This sense of owing their very existence to the game is a recurring theme. '*PUBG* has given me everything,' says Mysterious YT. She spends eight hours a day playing and streaming *PUBG*—about as much as a full-time job. 'Being a streamer is not easy; I may look active in front of the camera, but I haven't slept. To tell you the truth, I haven't slept well in six months. Ever since I started streaming, I haven't slept well.' Sleepless nights notwithstanding, Mysterious YT feels indebted to *PUBG*. 'I could die for *PUBG*, it's like that,' she says.[21]

Endless Worlds, Infinite Possibilities

I used to spend hours reading when I was your age, we chide iGen as we pry the video game controller from their reluctant hands. Every generation of parents has attempted a caste system of leisure activity which the next generation has successfully demolished. iGen stands ready to dismiss our suggestions, recognizing that many fantasy worlds from books made real by the alchemy of our imaginations are now to be found on the game screen. *The Hitchhiker's Guide to the Galaxy* has simply metamorphosized from the printed page to a mesmerizing game with phenomenal visuals and world-class soundtracks. From book adaptations to car racing and city planning, the world of gaming has a mind-boggling number of genres to satisfy every palate. Just in case you are uninitiated in the gaming world, here are some popular examples that you can use as a cheat sheet when you talk to your kids:

Real-time Strategy Games (*Age of Empires*, *Warcraft* and *Plants vs Zombies* among others): These games have complex quests that usually involve building armies, allocating resources wisely to expand territories and gaining victory through technological advancements. Notably, many of these games, including Age of Empires, have been lauded for sparking an interest in history and providing a 'crash course' in material economics.

Role-play Games (*World of Warcraft*, *Dota 2*, *League of Legends*, *Diablo* and *Dark Souls* among others): These real-time games are played on cloud-based servers and have quests that test the gamers' ability to service the game with their chosen hero. Many games in this genre hold multiple world records, such as the largest multiplayer platform (*World of Warcraft*) and the richest e-sports tournament (*Dota 2* with a prize of $47 million for the winner).

Platform Games (*Super Mario Bros, Sonic the Hedgehog, Castlevania, Temple Run* and *Subway Surfer* among others): Many of these games are instantly recognizable to iGen parents and are often referred to as 'classics'. Based on dexterously moving from one destination to the others, some of the games in this list have successfully been expanded into Hollywood and Netflix series.

Puzzle games (*Candy Crush Saga, Wordle, Tetris, Tekken, Street Fighter* and *Shadow Fight* among others): Aiming to pick gamers' brains on a puzzle matrix, games like *Candy Crush Saga* hold several records, including being among the most downloaded games ever. These are also known as the reason you stay up all night.

Open World Shooter Games (*PUBG, Grand Theft Auto, Hitman* and *Counter-Strike* among others): These games focus on a first-person playable character, with *PUBG* and *Counter-Strike* becoming some of the most streamed games in the history of gaming.

Racing Games (*Asphalt* and *Need for Speed* among others): These games involve completing races across various terrains and difficulties while collecting the most coveted car models in your races.

Some research indicates that spending time playing games each week can increase brain activity, and, in particular, boost the cognitive skills required for decision-making.[22] First-person shooter games like *PUBG*, in particular, require gamers to pay close attention at all times, making split-second decisions that could mean the difference between virtual life or death. Perhaps this is why players of first-person shooter games report improved spatial reasoning and decision-making skills.[23] Studies reveal that after an hour of video game play, gamers had improved visual selective attention and showed positive changes in brain activity.[24]

Not so *kharab* after all.

The New Nawabs

2020 was the year when droves of engineers got laid off and doctors lost whatever work-life balance they had due to the mortal grip the pandemic had over the world. In the same year, the gaming industry made $155 billion in revenue. By 2022, the industry's revenues had surged past the $200 billion mark making gaming bigger than Hollywood and the music industry combined. The gaming industry now employs millions of designers, artists, musicians, scriptwriters, marketing gurus, salespersons, public relations managers and programmers. Whatever skills your child possesses—from physics to public relations—the gaming industry is likely to require them.

Apart from the professionals who work on the backend of gaming, it's becoming increasingly clear that there is a new kind of *nawab* in town: gaming vloggers. The ten richest gamers in the world all have net worths that runs into millions (and most of them aren't even thirty yet!) Perhaps it's useful to pause the game here and place gamers into two broad categories: e-sports players who compete professionally and streamers who game for content creation. Both categories have witnessed massive growth in recent years and are demonstrably becoming viable career options for iGen. For instance, the average e-sports player in India earns between Rs 40,000 and Rs 75,000 per month not including prize money and sponsorships. Top-rated players will make considerably more with a salary that ranges between Rs 1 to Rs 1.5 lakh per month.[25] This is in addition to any sponsorships that may help them monetize their brand, which Indian gamers such as Tanmay Singh aka Scout, have done successfully. Perhaps the point was best made by CarryMinati when he joined Tom Cruise on the red carpet after inking a deal with Paramount Pictures to promote the *Mission: Impossible* film series. Who said gaming couldn't take you to impossible places?

Then there are the streamers. iGen is quickly moving away from watching traditional sports on television, preferring to watch gamers play on YouTube and Twitch. And as competitive gaming circuits increase across India, there has been an explosion of gaming influencers in India who livestream their gameplay for audiences. There's money to be made here too. According to reports, a well-managed channel by a popular Indian streamer with nearly ten million subscribers could end up making close to a million dollars a year. Admittedly, these are rarefied circles, but the numbers are encouraging even in the more achievable target range of 3,00,000–5,00,000 subscribers. Streamers with fewer than half a million subscribers can still earn up to $1,00,000 a year.[26] As the money begins to pile up and educational institutions start to offer classes in gaming, many in iGen are considering video gaming as a viable career. According to reports,[27] nearly half of India's gamers want to pursue gaming as a career, a number that beats both the US and Japan!

The Double-Edged Sword

But in gaming, just as in life, everyone isn't always a winner. Gaming, like most tech products, is a double-edged sword, with addiction being the sharp side that has sliced through many lives. Gamers have broken their thumbs from overuse; some have forgotten to eat, while others consistently lie to their bosses and skip work to play games instead.* Some of us almost skip our weddings. In a now-viral video clip, a groom sits on the *mandap* of his wedding ceremony unable to look up. He's holding his phone and furiously playing *PUBG* while his bemused and may I add, rather forgiving bride looks on. While this clip was entertaining, other incidents have been far more sinister.

A seventeen-year-old boy from Haryana was rebuked by his parents for his *PUBG* addiction. His mother took away his phone to stop him from playing. He died of suicide the next morning.[28] Furqan Qureshi, a sixteen-year-old boy from Bhopal, collapsed after playing *PUBG* for several hours. Furqan's sister Fiza watched helplessly as Furqan suddenly began shouting, 'Blast it . . . blast it . . .' before collapsing on the bed. 'The excitement of the video game might have caused a surge in adrenaline, causing increased heart rate and cardiac arrest,' said the cardiologist who treated Furqan.[29] Recently, a fitness

---

* South Korea has the most tired gamers, with 66.8 per cent missing sleep while gaming. Germany seems to have the hungriest with 43.6 per cent of gamers missing a meal to play video games. We seem to be the most truant nation with over 24 per cent of Indian gamers skipping work to game.

trainer had to be hospitalized. He had been playing *PUBG* continuously for several days when he started hitting himself, thinking that he was still on the battlefield. With games getting ever more immersive, perhaps it's unsurprising that the seams between online and reality are beginning to wear thin.

According to experts, eight out of ten technology addiction cases worldwide are related to gaming. It's a concern that has many nations worried and with gaming addiction skyrocketing, the WHO officially classified 'gaming disorder' as a medical condition. Countries such as China have imposed age restrictions on gamers under the age of eighteen allowing them to play only for an hour on weekends and statutory holidays. Of course, China isn't the only country with a problem. For this section, I interviewed gamers from across India all of whom were between the ages of ten and thirty, most of them male. Across the age ranges, these interviews stood out:

Ayaan, Fourteen, New Delhi

Ayaan attends a prestigious South Delhi school where he captains the football team. We're in his family's farmhouse on the outskirts of Delhi. The lights have been dimmed in the room because Ayaan and his video games have taken over. 'Everyone, all my friends, play *GTA*. It's like the coolest game,' says Ayaan as we settle down. He may be right about the 'everyone plays it' part; the game has generated over $8 billion in revenue since its launch. I point out that *GTA (Grand Theft Auto)* is rated 'M' for 'Mature Audiences' but Ayaan is in player mode, in more ways than one. Busty, skimpily-clad women flit across the screen, clearly prostitutes. Helpfully, one of them has 'skank' tattooed across her backside. Ayaan drives through breezily, throwing money at one woman and contemplating the sexual favours offered by another as he navigates the violence and drug deals that seem to be central to this game. I'm baffled. My young friend, though, seems unfazed.

Gaurav, Sixteen, Mumbai

I heard about Gaurav through Dr Shah, a psychologist based in Mumbai. Gaurav used to be a typical twelve-year-old with typical grades and typical hobbies—cricket and football. He began playing video games two years ago and was instantly drawn to it. At first, there was nothing extraordinary to report except that he really enjoyed his gaming sessions. But over the next few months, he started to refuse to leave his room—he needed to play. Food had to be served in front of a screen if it was to be eaten at all. He had stopped brushing his teeth regularly and bathing had become a biweekly affair. I asked why. 'He said brushing his teeth meant that he had two minutes less to play the game,' Dr Shah replies. Gaurav soon started refusing to attend school and instead alternated between the three screens in his room: the television, iPad and desktop computer. He was averaging sixteen hours of gaming every day. 'Basically, he only existed to play games online,' says his mother. The school counsellor tried to help but ultimately referred him to a psychologist. 'He was caught in a web of negative emotions and often needed a doctor to calm him down,' Dr Shah explains. When I met him, Gaurav hadn't been to school in three months.

Saurav, Twenty-One, Bengaluru

Much of my initial knowledge about *PUBG* came from competitive gamer Saurav, a helpful young man from Bengaluru. Saurav has spent long hours on video calls with me showcasing different aspects of the game. When we finally meet in Bengaluru, he is continually reaching for pain relief cream to rub on his wrists. 'The burn is worth it,' he tells me when I pointedly look at the cream. 'Oh man! That feeling when you win the game, it's like you're on top of the world,' he continues. But he knows that there's another side. 'When I was in college, I would start playing at 8 a.m. and would continue until 3 a.m. the next day. I had more online friends than I did in real life. My online gaming friends, whom I had never met before, were more aware of my problems than my roommate. I realized I had a problem when my ex-girlfriend broke up with me after years of this,' he says.

While conducting these interviews, I begin to appreciate one thing: the worlds created by *GTA*, *PUBG* and other games are haunting. The experience is seductive. It's no surprise that kids can barely tear themselves away from it. Who can resist the phenomenally realistic visuals, world-class soundtracks and glamorized violence in which you get to swagger on as the hero? Speaking of glamorized violence, it's important to note here that many of the examples cited in this section have focused on *PUBG* simply because of the proportion of iGen who play this game almost exclusively. Perhaps CarryMinati was right when he said, '*PUBG ne poora scene hee change kar diya*' and yet, this focus on *PUBG* should not undermine the fact that other games are equally addictive. In fact, addiction isn't the exclusive domain of one game. Just ask any alcoholic, it's never about one kind of vodka. The massively popular *World of Warcraft* is often dubbed 'World of Warcrack' in reference to its addictive nature. *Fortnite*, a quick-fire game that creates high-pressure situations, is also the source of many addictions. It doesn't matter whether you're pumping bullets in Fortnite or whirling around to complete a magical quest in the kingdom of Azeroth—every game is designed to make you chase a high.

William Siu is a successful mobile game developer whose games have generated over a billion dollars in sales. Recently, he wrote an op-ed piece for the *New York Times* provocatively titled 'I Make Video Games. I Won't Let My Daughters Play Them,' an article that I insisted my own daughter should read. Siu goes on to rationalize his parenting decision by revealing that game addiction is laced into every game's basic product design. 'I hired product managers and engineers to track everything players did and analyze their behaviour. Using the data we collected, we experimented with every feature of our games to see which versions allowed us to extract the most time and money from our players. For us, game addiction was by design: It meant success for our business,' says Siu.[30] Classic *dil maange more*.

So, what's a parent to do? E-sports will now feature in the Commonwealth Games with participants competing for medals in three different video games. There are strong lobbying efforts to include video games in the Olympics. Almost 200 higher education institutions in the US offer varsity e-sports programmes, complete with scholarships.[31] Are these educational opportunities or gateway drugs to tech addiction? Could they be alternate career goldmines for our children? Each family will have to decide for itself.

In the meantime, I have installed Steam, the online game downloading platform and *Dota 2* is downloading on my laptop. After all, turning forty is about trying new things. I may not become a professional gamer, but I'll enjoy spending time with my children as their teammates. Perhaps that's the only way to win this particular game.

Level Up: How to Become a Player in iGen's Game

'To game or not to game? That is [today's] question!' Well, for starters, there's nothing inherently good or bad about gaming. In fact, deciding whether or not to game is much like gaming itself: you need to make tactical decisions with limited knowledge. As you decide, it's worth considering how closely gaming aligns with your child's life goals. How might it benefit your kid? The answer is usually a combination of social opportunities, career options and learning all mixed in with good old-fashioned fun. A real deck of trumps! With so many trumps not to mention a tremendously sticky product design, gaming becomes that classic double-edged knife capable of slicing through even the most sensible kid. But as parents, we didn't hand our children the kitchen knife before teaching them how to use it safely. The same logic applies to gaming. For their own safety, our kids need to learn how to use this knife and here are a few strategies to keep it from cutting to the quick:

1) **Watch the clock:** Official bodies in several countries, including the American Academy of Paediatrics, recommend limiting gaming to one hour per day. Post-pandemic, children in India are spending an average of almost four hours per day playing video games![32] However, just as countries have differing views on gaming limits, so will every family. Choose a reasonable time limit that works for your family and do your best to stick to it. Remember, you're dealing with a hugely addictive product design and therefore, the deck is stacked against you as far as setting boundaries is concerned. Older mediums (like this book) have built-in cues such as the end of a chapter which signal natural stopping points. Video games, on the other hand, are virtually bottomless. Set yourself up for success as you attempt to make your kid stick to the time limit. For instance, you might avoid giving your kid a closed room or 'den' to play in. Remember, some animals will spend months in their den!

2) **Become a playa! (yes, you can!):** As daunting as it may seem, most games are designed for maximum appeal which means that if you try, you can play. We've all played endless rounds of Snakes and Ladders with our kids, and this is another opportunity to be on the same gameboard as them, taking turns through the wins and losses. Besides, gaming together provides a crucial opportunity that Snakes and Ladders cannot: the chance to set boundaries in the virtual world. Gaming

invariably involves interacting with anonymous avatars, many of whom will abuse or bully other players with impunity. Harassment and 'doxing' (sharing private information online) are rife on every gaming platform as are predators who may use the game to groom younger players. Perhaps they'll give them a coveted coin or maybe they'll suggest a private coaching session, anything to win your kid's trust. When you encounter harassment or predatory behaviour while playing video games with your kid, you have the opportunity to demonstrate how to handle the situation. Since you're in the game too, you can help your child identify red flags and set boundaries so that they are able to deal with the situation independently later. Remember how you cycled alongside your kid when they were first learning how to ride a bike? Well, it's time to do it all over again. They'll be better equipped to navigate the streets on their own once they've learned how to deal with aggressive oncoming traffic.

3) **Socialize IRL:** Your kid will interact with existing friends while gaming and likely also make new ones. But things begin to slide down a slippery slope when gaming becomes the primary way to socialize. Varun, fifteen, says his parents often tell him to turn off the game. 'But I tell them that I can't because it's the only socializing I do,' he says. It's much easier to put down the gaming console when you can have adventures outside of the game.

4) **Stay clean:** Practicing 'gaming hygiene' doesn't just mean forcing your kid to shower (although that's crucial too!). Minimize blue light exposure and don't allow gaming before bedtime as both practices can dramatically interfere with sleep. It is critical that your child takes physical breaks to move their muscles and rest their eyes. Several games can help you achieve this by auto-pausing every thirty minutes, giving the kid time to rest and recover before re-entering this alternate universe.

If there's a Problem . . .

For most kids, gaming is something they do alongside other activities such as playing sports, studying and hanging out with friends. But for a growing number of kids, playing video games comes at the cost of everything else. 'I wanted to climb inside the game and breathe there. I wanted to live there and die there,' said Saurav during our interview. It's hard to hear your kid talk like this and if you do, your instinct might be to ban the game altogether. But think twice before throwing the gaming console out of the house; an insufferably hard line with zero tolerance will simply force your kid to game elsewhere or play when he thinks you're not looking. Start slowly and be specific. Level with your child and let them know that you're beginning to question gaming's alignment with the family's values. You could say: 'You become aggressive and angry when I ask you to turn off the game. I've spoken to your teachers, and it's clear that you're finding it difficult to concentrate in class.' And then instead of throwing the console out the window, offer a new, more reasonable rule that might include setting a time limit or playing only on certain days of the week.

But as your kid reduces their gaming, they might find themselves 'stuck' with endless swathes of time. Gaming is the ultimate time-suck and not having a game to vacuum up time can be disconcerting. Consider the simple 1:2 rule instituted by my friend Kriti's parents when we were growing up. Every time we asked to watch television, her parents reminded us that we had to play outside for two hours before being given the remote for an hour. 1:2. It remains a simple rule to follow that strikes a balance while combating excess. But despite Kriti's parent's clever hack, you'll likely encounter your kid saying they are bored without video games. Bored with a capital B. All. The. Time. Don't (insensitively) insist that they use this newfound time to study or read a book: it won't work! Help them come up with a fun new hobby that is also cool, maybe learning how to DJ or play basketball. Gaming requires a significant investment of time and if they quit without replacing it with another interesting hobby, the game will just seduce them back in.

Unfortunately, the time suck won't be the only issue that you have to contend with as a parent of a gamer who is trying to quit. Quite apart from the admirable job that it does in vacuuming up time, many kids find gaming addictive because it seems to demonstrate measurable progress. As they level-up, collect more coins and kill more enemies, gamers feel that they're progressing because the game consistently rewards them as they move past the challenges. It sends a strong signal to the gamer's brain; *I'm getting better at something* they think.

Quantifiable progress is an addictive feeling and while pivoting from gaming, you could challenge your child to progress in life instead. Distribute progression through life's goals and collect coins along the way. Learning to play the guitar could be a bronze coin, improving their diet could be a silver coin and together you can think of something spectacular that qualifies for gold. Your praise and support will replace the digital trophies so keep them coming.

In all of this, go easy on yourself. There will be moments when you believe your efforts deserve a gold medal. They probably do. But take solace in the fact that you are not alone: this is a worldwide issue unique to the times we live in. Just as there are billions of gamers who are turning on their gaming consoles right now, there are also millions who are trying to quit.

CHAPTER SEVEN

PARADOX OF PROTECTION: THE CONSEQUENCE OF OVERPARENTING IGEN

Helicoptering through Life

Delivery doesn't stop at delivery; long after we leave the maternity wing at the hospital, we're still trying to deliver the perfect child. For many in our generation, parenting has become the all-consuming, full-time job that we often juggle alongside our other consuming, full-time jobs. We *do* parenting. We parent like crazy. We parent hard. We sign up for parenting classes with experts who profess to have the recipe for raising the perfect kid, optimally calibrated for academic, sporting and personal success buttressed by perfect manners and a personality that is both amiable and competitive in exactly the right proportions. Mandarin sessions need to be balanced with piano classes and as we make the kids practice chokeholds in jiu-jitsu class we feel like we're in the Parenting Hunger Games ourselves. 'Team sports build teamwork, but solo sports build leadership,' we breathlessly insist as our children huff along to both football camp *and* tennis lessons. Every year, my friend Karina attempts to 'future-proof' her son by insisting he attends the hottest coding camps in town. He's been learning Java, C++ and Python since he was eight years old. I ask Karina why she insists on these camps despite his protests that grow louder every year. 'It helps him concentrate,' she replies. 'Like a concentration camp.' Even though I work with words, I'm struck speechless.

The race often begins before our children can take their first steps. We make them listen to Mozart in utero and dash through trivia flashcards in their first few months in the hope that they will be sorting isosceles and equilateral triangles by the time they are toddlers. Fuelled by both comparisons and competitions, our lives become a never-ending Pinterest board of animal-shaped sandwiches, Suzuki violin lessons and enrichment activities. We expend every spare ounce of energy trying to anticipate our children's needs, pausing breathlessly to congratulate ourselves if we are able to offer them something—an experience, a toy, an activity—before they even know they want it. If a sports kit or class diary is left at home, we rush it to school before the child can miss it. We pretend to do homework *with* them and often end up doing it *for* them while checking in with the teacher to ensure that 'everything is on track'.

'My Parents Didn't Know Which Class I Was in'

Our overparenting couldn't be more different from the 'benign neglect' that was often the hallmark of our childhoods. Most of us ran around eating as much cake as our mouths could fit, playdates didn't have timings, and no one checked to see if the apples were organic. We were deeply loved but we weren't strictly monitored.

I recently asked my mother how she prepared for my first day at school. 'I didn't do much. Just made sure your hair was combed, your uniform was on and off you went,' she replied. Today, many of urban India's 'top nurseries' require an orthopaedic check-up, an ophthalmologist sign-off, an ENT report and a full panel of blood work before admitting a perfectly healthy child to the premises. My child is applying to one of these institutions, which requires all of the above as well as three essays outlining how I intend to contribute to my child's success and the nursery's prowess. I spend such long hours working on these forms that I am reminded of my master's degree programme application. Even though the most academically advanced activity in this school is making Play-Doh elephants, the application process feels mind-numbingly onerous with multiple forms to be filled out, complex opinion pieces to write and several rounds of interviews to sit through. After all of this work, I can't help but feel that my child's success is mine to engineer and a few weeks later when the nursery sends a rejection letter, I feel like *I* have failed.

I tell my aunt about my failure, and she responds with a hysterical laugh. 'When I was in school, if you had asked my parents which class I was in, they probably wouldn't have known. I mean, they would have had a general idea, but they wouldn't have known whether it was the sixth or seventh standard exactly.' She clearly thinks I'm overinvolved, and in turn, I find her dismissiveness annoying. I ask her, a little sharply, if she thinks her parents didn't value education all that much. 'No, it wasn't that,' she replies evenly, 'it's just that everything was much more relaxed back then.' I struggle to understand her nonchalance, especially since I receive a daily email detailing exactly which sums and spellings were taught in my daughter's class that day as well as how many jumping jacks were done during the PE lesson. I know every inflection of my kid's academic progress and often end up saying things like, 'Let's get to bed early tonight. We have school tomorrow.' I also know that I'm not alone. Recently, when I suggested to a friend that we meet for a coffee, she told me that she couldn't leave the house because she had to spend the week completing her child's art project. By the time it was done, it could have put the Mona Lisa to shame.

But who can blame our enthusiasm to protect our children when human overparenting seems to be nature's intention? Elephant calves are strong enough to walk with the herd within hours of being born, and baby giraffes can flee from predators before the sun sets on their first day. Human babies, on the other hand, are among the most helpless offsprings in the natural world. Let's be honest, they're not exactly born smart. Forget standing upright, they can't even turn on their sides, and speaking is a long way off when you can't even burp unassisted. These helpless creatures would perish within hours if we didn't intervene. If our babies are to survive, we need to prevent danger and so, our species is hardwired to be exquisitely tuned to our children's needs. However, while overparenting is our initial genetic impulse, trouble brews when we don't rewire our instincts to allow our children to walk with the herd and flee from predators on their own legs once they can. Instead of letting them eventually roam free as nature intended, we hover above in helicopters as they limp their way through the savannah.

The Adult in the Crib

My friend Neeva and her husband Ajay call to seek my advice on college applications. Wait, I should clarify: Neeva and Ajay are both in their late forties, and neither is off to college. This call is on behalf of their seventeen-year-old daughter, Vani. When I suggest that Vani call me herself, I hear Neeva exhale sharply. I continue to insist on speaking directly with Vani, but Neeva and Ajay push back. 'We're pretty much writing her application for her anyway!' they say with a laugh. Vani eventually gets on the phone, but Neeva joins the call within a few minutes. 'Let me give you the names of the colleges that we've shortlisted so far. I don't like cold weather, so we've avoided all of those places,' she explains.

'But maybe Vani doesn't mind the cold?' I ask.

Neeva laughs off my question. 'But hello! I'll be going too!' she replies as Vani stays silent. Neeva intends to partially relocate to the city where her daughter will attend college. Instead of living in a college dorm room, Vani will most likely share an apartment with her mother. An adult in a crib.

As part of my research, I interviewed several parents whose children had left for college in other cities and countries. Some parents had memorized the layout of the college campus and routinely advised their child on the best walking path to a particular building. Others were overseeing course enrolments and insisting professors pay special attention to their kids. One mother was concerned that her nineteen-year-old son was finding the chairs in the class uncomfortable, while another planned to call her daughter's roommate's mother to discuss how the girls should share the room. My own family isn't far behind. My cousin tells me that when it was time to come home from college for the holidays, her father would calculate—down to the minute—what time she had to leave campus in order to make it to the airport in time. 'He would wake up in the middle of the night in Mumbai to make sure I'd left for the airport in Boston.' This cousin is now thirty years old, married, and has a child of her own. Her father still calls to make sure that she has left for the airport on time.

There are many parenting experts out there, but bestselling author Julie Lythcot–Haimes is an expert on *over*parenting. Julie has served as dean of freshmen at Stanford University which gives her unique insight into how overparenting affects iGen. Julie and I are on the phone as she explains her theory. 'Most parents are raising either delicate orchids or prized racehorses,' she says. Orchids, she explains, need constant care and protection, they're delicate beings that can only survive in the perfectly calibrated environment of the greenhouse, not in the real world. I think back to how we carefully complete our child's homework for them, rush a forgotten PE kit to school and hand out participation trophies so that no one's feelings are hurt. Orchids. On the other hand, racehorses have blinders on and are relentlessly driven to goals that are specified by a parent. The finish lines are ostensibly different but share the typical markers of success: an impossible-to-get-into college, a high-paying job with a fancy title or a clutch of degrees. Racehorses typically don't reach a final finish line since the reward of achievement is often the next achievement. Racehorse pressure is immense, and it often drives iGen to unacceptable lengths; as I write this, several WhatsApp groups are talking about a student at an elite Mumbai school who faked his US university application by claiming credit for work he did not do and leadership positions he never held. Entire cities in India, such as Kota, are teeming with racehorse kids living out their parents' version of success and running never-ending races towards finish lines that were never theirs to begin with. I am speaking to a forty-year-old friend—successful in his own right—who says he still feels guilty about having disappointed his parents by not following the family career. I gently remind him that his path is different, but my words don't seem to matter—the whips on racehorses last long and run deep.

The Tale of the Cellphone and Helicopter

Social media is so rife with comparisons and competition that it often fuels the overparenting pandemic. We find ourselves on the quest to raise the perfect child: fed on organic vegetables, speaking fluent Mandarin and delivering virtuoso violin performances on their way to top-tier universities. This is almost impossible to achieve without hovering over our children but what would have required near-constant physical presence in the past is now easily achieved by our phones. Technology may not have invented helicopter parenting but it certainly makes the hovering easier. In fact, it presents yet another paradox: the same phones that allow our children more freedom than any generation before them are the very devices that allow us to overparent like no other generation.

With technology, parents have visibility on their children's every move. 'WHERE are you and WHO are you with?' we roar into our phones. And just like kids exchange memes, parents swap info on the latest surveillance app. 'Hi everyone, Plz share your favourite apps for tracking kids,' writes a friend on one of my larger parenting WhatsApp groups. This particular group has almost 200 members and the question seems to elicit almost as many responses with parents tripping over each other to nominate their favourite snoop app. The overwhelming frontrunner seems to be Life360. In photography, a 360-degree camera has a field of view that covers the entire sphere and as its name suggests, Life360 gives you an omnidirectional field of view on your kid's life. It tells you everything from their current location to how fast they are driving. I am talking to Kanika who uses it to track her college-aged son. 'It's a great app,' she says. 'I know exactly where he is at all times. Once he tried to turn his location off, but the app immediately sent me a notification that GPS was being turned off. I called him immediately. And he can't even tell me that his battery ran out because the app sends me a notification if his battery is running low.' I ask if she calls her son to remind him to charge his phone. 'All the time. I'm fully stalking my kid!' she replies.

It's not just their physical location, technology also gives us the ability to track their every academic move. My daughter's school provides parents with a portal and two apps that allow us to follow our child's academic progress in real-time. But all this information comes at a cost: teachers must spend hours during an already busy day uploading photos, test scores and lesson plans to these portals. 'The school day has always been packed, but now it's totally manic. I feel like I'm under pressure to record every moment. Half the time I end up asking myself, "Should I use this time to teach the kids or to upload updates for parents?"' says a secondary school teacher at my child's school. Because of the constant uploads, I usually know my daughter's test scores before she can inform me herself. This often ends up having an unintended consequence. Now that I am being drip-fed these scores, I feel like I must *do* something with them. This quicksand of granular information sucks me into micromanaging my kid, so I email teachers for every insignificant academic dip. My mind doesn't know what to make of this data (that I probably shouldn't be receiving), and so I email the teacher again. And she has to make the time to reply to me. Again.

Whether it's Live360 or parent portals, many of us are saturated with data on our children but continue to add to the load. I am visiting my friend Aman when she informs me that I am being watched. 'You're under surveillance. But don't worry! It's not just you,' she laughs as I shift from one foot to another, looking both cornered and concerned. 'Everyone in my house is being watched. I believe in using technology with all its features!' Aman goes on to explain that there are infrared thermal cameras set up in every room of the house, including all the bedrooms. 'I know which door has opened in which room and who went to the bathroom at what time,' she says.[*] I look on in amazement as Aman uses Alexa to first 'drop into' the living room to check on her son and then into her daughter's bedroom. Her daughter has a friend over and Aman wants to know what the two

_____

[*] I should mention here that no one in Aman's house deals with any sort of security risk.

girls are discussing. As things stand, they're discussing cupcake flavours and their class teacher. Nothing worth monitoring but Aman continues to listen in. I'm curious to know if she's looking for something in particular, so I ask her whether the surveillance has ever revealed anything remarkable. 'No, not really. It hasn't. But that doesn't mean that I'll stop watching. My only problem is with Aryan. He already knows how to turn off the camera systems,' she replies. But even as Aryan tampers with the camera systems, he continues to text his mother with updates. In fact, both the children send their mother constant updates because they know Aman's penchant for keeping in touch via technology. Later that night, Aman checks her phone for a minute-by-minute log of the day's activity in the house: who entered which room, what time the TV was turned on and when her kids last went to the bathroom. She studies the log every night before going to bed. 'I need to know,' Aman says firmly, 'it helps me feel connected.'

Connection, that elusive phenomenon! Satellites in the sky let us follow the exact route of the bus as it takes them to school. Parent portals in schools show us every sum they work out in math class. We download snoop apps while placing GPS devices and cameras everywhere. But as we monitor our kids' every step, are we creating more disconnection than ever? In the ultimate paradox, research[1] indicates that kids who indulged in the riskiest behaviour online were those whose parents physically monitored their online activities! One study[2] notes that the more parents called their teenage children, the more the teens responded with lies and half-truths. But when the kids themselves made the calls to their parents, they tended to be more honest. Perhaps when parents are being too intrusive, teens feel cornered or mistrusted and end up hiding their behaviour.[3] I speak to a teenager in Chennai about this, who tells me that she is more likely to 'bullshit' her parents when they call her on the phone and ask her where she is. I ask her why. 'I don't know,' she replies slowly. 'It just feels like they're interrogating me.'

The Perils of Prying

As we snoopervise our kids in an effort to keep them from making mistakes, we bubble wrap them as though they were baubles made of the most fragile glass. But this bubble-wrapped protection has its consequences, especially as adolescents approach adulthood. 'When kids grow, along with physical changes, there are also psychological milestones such as learning from mistakes. When kids are constantly monitored, they don't learn how to learn from their mistakes which impact their ability to connect with themselves,' explains Dr Shah. Her observations are backed by large studies: college students who use their phones to be constantly connected to parents tend to be less autonomous.[4]

When we do everything for our children—wake them up, send forgotten items to school, set alarms for flights, argue when a teacher gives feedback, step in when a friend is being aloof—we rob them of the chance to experience discomfort. And because they've been so *comfortable* their entire lives, they struggle with failure when it arrives simply because they've never had practice holding it or mapping its contours. Parents have always inoculated their children against disease, but today many of us are desperately trying to inoculate them against any danger, despair or disappointment, no matter how innocuous.

By bestowing upon us babies who cannot burp autonomously, nature may have tricked us into believing that we need to constantly have one hand on their backs, patting them forever. But we can't—and shouldn't— remain 'hands-on' for life. When parents make student art projects look like the Mona Lisa, this inadvertently raises the bar on expectations from students while making kids internalize that most damning of messages: 'my effort isn't good enough'. By ensuring that the kids never fail a test or lose a race we deprive them of critical growth opportunities. This, of course, becomes a self-fulfilling prophecy: because we haven't removed the bicycle training wheels, they are unable to pedal through life which forces us to screw the training wheels on even tighter.

I recently attended my daughter's primary school's sports day. As things stand, she isn't particularly Usain Bolt-y and didn't win a race. And yet, before we left the grounds, she was called on stage to receive a trophy along with the rest of the non-Usains. Every single child who attended sports day received a prize, regardless of their performance. While handing out participation trophies certainly spared some bruised egos, this kind of coddling can also help explain the record levels of entitlement amongst iGen. A landmark study from Columbia University revealed that kids who are constantly told they are smart (or fast!) tend to avoid activities in which they do not excel, essentially avoiding any possibility of failure.

This nagging fear of failure, the sinking feeling that your efforts aren't good enough and the constant need to have someone's hand on your back all add up. During my chat with Julie, she revealed that when administrators from top US colleges convene, they don't just discuss their students' academic achievements or future job prospects. The number one agenda item at these meetings is often *student mental health*. We have either made our children so fragile (remember the orchids) or stressed them out so much (recall the racehorses) that administrators are worrying about them jumping off bridges. Orchids or racehorses, either way, what we're often left with are vulnerable kids wandering the digital wastelands and anxiety-ridden parents who are increasingly disconnected from them. No one wants to hear it, but the current student suicide rate in India is at an all-time high, with more than one student dying every hour. That's a problem.

Snoopy Isn't a Good Look on Us

Unfortunately, many of us feel like jumping off bridges too: *today's parents suffer from depression at twice the rate of the general population.* 'I'm just trying to take it one day at a time and not lose my sh*t,' says a friend while we're at dinner. Many parents in the group nod sympathetically. We've all been there. Something about the way we are parenting is pushing us over the edge. It could be because many of us tend to believe that every single thing we do *really* matters, and so we don't give anyone a break, including ourselves. Several studies have examined the relationship between helicopter parenting and parent mental health and discovered consistent findings: the more 'intense' you are about parenting, the worse your mental health is likely to be. Other studies suggest that it's not just mental: our physical bodies are disintegrating too, with overly empathetic parents showing signs of accelerated cellular aging.[5] Our bodies are literally falling apart with stress. 'Intense' means different things to different people, but truth be told, we all know an intense parent when we see one. Many of us have been one.

Of course, the bazaar is only too happy to pump up our intensity and boost our anxiety. Anxious parents are among the most exploitable audiences in the world (although I am very grateful you've bought this book!). Want your child to be smarter? Better? Happier? Faster? Listen to our podcast. Download our app. From iPotty apps that help you plot every poop to college counsellors who write your child's essays, there are entire marketplaces dedicated to overparenting. I recently met a mother who was concerned about her toddler's picky eating. 'Then I found this new kinetic sand that replicates the feel of *roti sabzi*,' she said. 'So now, I spend an hour every day doing kinetic sand play with my daughter so she can enjoy holding food,' she said as her toddler attempted to eat mud.

Parents, especially mothers today have more educational and professional opportunities than ever before. Many of us enter childrearing after or in addition to full-time jobs, and we tend to pour all of our skills into parenting. But when we approach parenting as a job that must be done perfectly, our children become our careers, and their accomplishments become the sum total of our success. By doing that we inadvertently set ourselves up for disappointment. The quality of our own lives becomes brittle. This ends up damaging our children, particularly our girls, who internalize our anxiety, often feeling anxious themselves. I can't think of anything more ironic.

Love and Limits: Steering the Helicopter

Perhaps this section could do with a caveat on privilege. It's apparent that overparenting is often a curse of the privileged, something that frequently exists in the air-conditioned rooms of the affluent. You can only send forgotten items to school when your kid has a school to send things to. But a privileged phenomenon is still a phenomenon. Kids who are raised in smothering, suffocating environments are experiencing record levels of anxiety; figuratively and sometimes literally, they cannot breathe. And so, it may be worthwhile to momentarily pause the Mandarin lessons and consider what kind of parents we're being. Privileged or not, is our overparenting hurting our kids more than helping? Developmental psychologists across the world agree that most parents fit into one of three parenting styles,* so you'll likely recognize yourself in one of these:

---

* Psychologists do recognize a fourth parenting style characterized by neglect and abuse, but I'm assuming the good folks who make the effort to read parenting books will find that style largely irrelevant.

Authoritarian (*my house, my rules*): Authoritarian parents typically raise 'racehorses', prioritizing obedience and respect over all else. Rules are important but the only explanation given for a rule is 'because it's The Rule.' These parents often lack emotional warmth but demand a great deal from their children.

Permissive (*whatever you want, whenever you want*): Permissive parents consider themselves their child's best friend and constantly shield them from failure. They thrive on being the 'genie in the bottle' who magically makes their child's every wish come true. Discipline and demands usually take a backseat in the permissive household as the delicate orchid child can do no wrong.

Authoritative (*let's work together*): Many psychologists regard this as the 'sweet spot' of parenting because it combines the authoritarian and the permissive styles. Borrowing from authoritarian parents, authoritative parents tend to set high expectations for their children but with some crucial differences: they explain the reasons for their rules, allow for failure and encourage their children to make independent choices. And taking a page from the handbook of permissive parents, authoritative parents are involved, emotionally responsive and warmly present in their children's lives. As a result, kids understand what is expected of them, put their best foot forward and are secure in the knowledge that mistakes are acceptable. Using this sweet spot as a guideline, there are several things we can do to avoid overparenting in a digital world:

1) Don't Snoopervise

Growing up in the 1990s, there were several popular songs that became our anthems—the sassier the better. 'I Want to Break Free' we crooned and soon moved on to insisting 'Let's Talk About Sex, Baby'. We'd sing these songs at fast-food joints in loud and off-key groups, much to the annoyance of other, more sophisticated diners. While several things have changed in the last few decades, much remains the same. No matter how many rovers we land on moon, teenagers will always be teenagers. Adolescence will always be a time to forge new identities, break free and yes, talk about sex, baby! When we interfere with an adolescent's need to feel physically and psychologically separate from us, we go against nature.

Thankfully, not everyone has infrared cameras installed in their children's bedrooms, but a staggering number of parents use parental control apps such as uknowkids, mamabear, minormonitor and others to keep their kids from accessing inappropriate content online. These are useful. Somewhat. Sometimes. If an app is your kids' only online safety net, it will fail you. It will also likely fail your kids. Zoya informs me that she is unable to research her report on Herman Melville's classic *Moby Dick* because the safe search installed on her school device doesn't like the last word of the book title! Even if the safety app was more intuitive, by the time you figure out how to ensure a safe experience for your kid on one platform, chances are that they will have moved on to something else.

Other parents who aren't using parental control apps might resort to that time-tested move that parents worldwide have relied on for generations—snooping! You might be tempted to covertly snoop on your kid's social media accounts, steal their phone when they're not looking and go through their messages like a rogue CIA agent. But this is iGen we're talking about! Your snoopervision will quickly be discovered, and your kid will (rightly) feel like you've been trying to catch them in the wrong. Ditch the authoritarian surveillance, but don't feel compelled to be entirely permissive either. Consider the authoritative alternative, the holy grail of middle paths. Discuss your concerns with your kid and let them know that you will be keeping an eye on things simply to help them navigate the online world. Assure them that *you're there to supervise, not snoopervise.* This empowers our kids and gives them the opportunity to demonstrate good behaviour instead of feeling like their parents are trying to catch them red-handed. It shifts the responsibility from you to your child, which is a good thing. If you need more convincing, remember that several studies show that no matter how much surveillance is in place, parents cannot protect and prevent beyond a certain point. The CIA style of snooping is ultimately doomed and learning how to make good decisions will always be a kid's best firewall.

2) Build Their Resilience

Gandhi. Michelangelo. Serena Williams. Think of anyone who has achieved much in their lives. It's almost certain that they worked for that level of cool, their mom didn't do it for them. If we want to raise happy, successful children, they will have to learn their own hustle and be their own safety nets. Instead of treating them like delicate teacups that might chip if dropped, consider telling them about your resilience. We've all fallen and gotten back up; the kids need to hear stories that showcase our grit, not necessarily our success. It will help them understand that it is okay to fail and that the road to success is a circuitous, complicated path with no maps and many bumps.

Years ago, my friend Amitabh told me a story about how his father sent him off to school. 'On Monday, Dad gave me Rs 20 and said, "This is all you have. Find your way to school." On Tuesday, he halved the budget and gave me Rs 10 for the same journey Wednesday was Rs 5. Come Thursday, Dad says, "Ok *beta*, you have no money. Find your way to school." It wasn't easy but I managed,' Amitabh says. This story has stayed with me for decades because it speaks of a parent's effort to build resilience in a kid who would otherwise have been cossetted. Deliberately introducing friction in our children's lives ('You have no money. Find your way to school.') seems unimaginable especially considering that we're busy tracking them on Life360 to make sure the route they're taking has no traffic and that they arrived on time. Placing AirTags on a child's school bag when they are toddlers is one thing but continuing to stalk an adolescent while they are navigating the world comes with consequences. 'I feel like I can't make my own decisions,' says a teenager whose parents use Life360. 'I'm not in control of my life and I don't think that this is healthy, either for my parents or me.'

Kids need to develop the skills to independently navigate their worlds, both online and offline. They must have their alarm bells go off when a friend screenshots something that makes them uncomfortable or when a partner pressures them to send a private photo. If we continue to set their alarm clocks, they will never wake up on their own. As the research suggests:

First, we do it *for* you.

Then we do it *with* you.

Then we *watch* you do it.

Then *you do it yourself.*

Instead, as desi parents, we often fall into a classic double bind. *Tu ne duniya nahi dekhi,* we tell our kids disparagingly. And then we don't let them see the *duniya.*

3) Embrace Their Wings

A few years ago, the book *Battle Hymn of the Tiger Mother* took the country by storm, perhaps because we recognized our Indian parenting instincts in the memoirs of a Chinese American mother. In the book, author Amy Chua lists out the rules that her daughters must follow: they must never 'attend a sleepover, have a play date, be in a school play, complain about not being in a school play, watch TV or play computer games, choose their extracurricular activities, get any grade less than an A, not be the No. 1 student in every subject except gym and drama, play any instrument other than the piano and violin, not play the piano or violin'. Add kathak to the mix and this could have been written by any number of Indian parents. But here's the thing: we can force our kids to play the piano, but we're unlikely to get A.R. Rahmans because when we parent like tigers, we end up raising sheep.

Let them rebel instead. Their first assertion of themselves will be with us. This will be the first time they pit individual liberty against collective thought. It's the first time they will break away from groupthink and start deciding for themselves instead of waiting for directions on what time to get up and where to go. If they are to find meaning in their own lives, they will have to break away from us. This break is worth celebrating. As overparenting expert Julie says, *we're trying to raise adults, not children.*

And just as our children learn to live separately from us, we'll have to invest in lives without them. Too many parents answer a simple 'how are you?' with a rundown of what's happening in their children's lives. And while it's always nice to hear about someone's kids, it doesn't answer the question. How are *you*?

CHAPTER EIGHT

WALK THE TALK

It's still dark outside when I wake up and pick up my phone. I know there are better things that I could reach for this early in the morning: a glass of lemon water, my meditation journal, perhaps my husband. But in some misguided attempt to get ahead of the next catastrophe, the train wreck that was 2020 has me compulsively reading the news as soon as I open my eyes. So, still wading through that sleepy, milky consciousness, I click on the country's top English news app. The first thing that I see on Trending Stories is 'HOW TO GET GISELE'S SUPERMODEL BODY!' I haven't even drawn the curtains to let the sun in, but notifications, negativity and noise are already making themselves at home in my head.

A few hours later, lemon brew finally in hand, I'm hanging out with my toddler who seems to find my company very dull. Either that or he has a complaint to lodge with his father. Probably both. 'Papa inside phone,' says Jahan, responding to the voice coming from the telephone. The brew seems bitter as I reflect on the accuracy of Jahan's words. Several times a day, it must feel like his parents *live inside their phones*. Later that day, I visit a friend's newborn and do another double take.[*] The six-month-old is wearing a onesie that reads 'Stop Texting and Feed Me'. It's turning out to be a day filled with signs.

As I draw the curtains closed for the night, my mind turns to a joke from a long time ago. I was having dinner with a few Harvard Medical School students who were

---

[*] To be clear, it isn't the baby's olfactory assault combined with the clearly imminent diaper explosion that frightens me. I've seen enough in my time.

laughing about how they would rather be dermatologists than cardiologists when they graduate. 'Maybe I'll pop zits instead of replacing hearts, but at least I won't get calls at midnight,' one of them chuckled.* This was back when dinosaurs roamed the Earth, and our phones were not yet extensions of our bodies. As we joked around that summer evening, no one—not even these brightest of minds—imagined that technology would have the last laugh. Today, whether you're a surgeon or a singer, it's virtually impossible to clock out of work. You don't need to have a life-saving job for emails, messages, notifications, beeps and pings to be the constant soundtrack to your life, even at midnight. We're all 'on call' after hours but then again, who even knows what the hours are anymore. The corporate honcho needs to immediately reply to every email; the influencer needs to be the first to post about the latest trend; the journalist needs to urgently tweet about the breaking news, and the rest of us need to immediately acknowledge every WhatsApp. And so, each of us becomes a contributor to a culture in which connectivity = success = connectivity. The ultimate infinite loop.

On the odd occasion that we do separate from our phones, it feels as though the world might implode. In turn, our children watch us go about our lives with this electronic leash around our necks, the youngest among them often mimicking our panic when they see us untethered. I'm at a friend's house when his four-year-old comes running over, clearly worried and clutching his father's phone. 'Papa,

---

* He went on to become a successful thoracic surgeon. I imagine he receives calls at midnight.

you're here but your phone is there,' the toddler says anxiously. 'Take it, take it, take it,' he repeats, pushing the phone into his father's hand. Leashed to their devices, our children are getting used to a new kind of parent.

A New Kind of Parent

It doesn't matter if you're in a car, on a train or 35,000 feet above the ground—you're leashed. The phone is a permanent guest at family dinners, school sports days, movie nights and even bedtime tuck-ins. It's there at concerts, funerals and everything in between. I sit down to do a jigsaw puzzle with Jahan but mindlessly check my phone while he hunts for the pieces. I look up to find him staring at me, and in that instant when our eyes meet, I can see what he's thinking. He's piecing together a different puzzle in his mind, perhaps that human beings cannot interact without technology. Because—and I say this with deep regret—kids don't do what we say, they do what we do. Sigh.

Given that our home isn't immune to the tech invasion, Zoya devised an experiment to see how long we could survive without our phones during Lockdown 1. It was a time when she could freely monitor the adults in the house making it the perfect setting for her experiment. Three of the four adults caved within the first hour and begged for their phones back. My mother was shocked when her granddaughter tracked her screen time and showed her the results.* We're quick to berate iGen for their phone

---

* Consider downloading apps like 'Moment' that help you track your screen time. Sometimes your phone can help you get off your phone.

addiction but occasionally they show us the mirror. The adults in our home didn't do a great job of contemplating their reflections and with our phones safely back in our hands, we continued with business as usual: a quick check on Instagram, a glance at an email and a scroll through the notifications, each break representing a shift in energy and attention. Almost every house has a similar story. A five-year-old tells me, despairingly, 'There's no one to tie my ponytail. Even nani is playing games on her phone.' Parenting today means giving our kids what the experts have termed 'continuous partial attention'.[1] Simply put, *a part of us is with our kids all the time but all of us is with them none of the time.*

One could argue that children have always had to deal with parents who were away perhaps working a till, tilling the land or just being somewhere that wasn't home. But the difference is that when those parents walked through the door, they were really home. That is no longer the case today. When we walk in the door, our phones walk in with us insisting that we reply to the email, check the Amazon orders and respond to the tenth joke of the day on the third family WhatsApp group. So, just as iGen presents us with a new parenting challenge, we present iGen with a new parent challenge: *how will the kids deal with us,* this new half-parent who is constantly distracted, frenzied and tuned-out?

For five years, Jenny Radesky, professor of paediatrics at the University of Michigan has studied the effects of parents being on their phones. Here's what she found: 'When parents' attention is directed at a smartphone, we talk to our children less, miss their bids for attention, overreact to their annoying interruptions, and think less clearly about what their behaviour means.'[2] I know exactly what Radesky means. When I'm on the phone, even if it's just a casual conversation, my kids' interruptions quickly escalate from annoying Level 5 to maddening Level 10. *Why am I being interrupted now?* I think to myself and sometimes out loud. *Why when I'm on the phone?* But the problem is that we're all always on the phone!

I interviewed children across the country to learn about their parents' phone habits. Rather than asking kids about their phone usage, I decided to ask about their parents' phone habits. About *our* phone habits, yours and mine. Many of the responses were difficult to digest because they held up a mirror to my own distractions. Suhana, thirteen, said, 'I feel bad because I feel like I'm always taking my mom away from something more interesting than me.' Kabir, fourteen, said, 'I have to compete for my parents' attention but it's really tough. How do I compete with a phone?' Kabir's response stayed with me for a while, and I spent considerable time researching and reflecting on that question. *How does a kid compete with a phone?*

Our current mindless use of technology is making us dumber, sadder and, in many cases, lonelier. It's also making us lousy parents. That's pretty ironic, given that we're spending more time worrying about our children than any previous generation. Could we be exemplifying the worst possible style of parenting—always present physically, thereby limiting children's autonomy, but only half present emotionally?[3] It's a frightening thought but even if we are, it's too early to declare a stalemate.

Resigning ourselves to this invasion will force our children to compete head-to-head with their parents' phones in an unwinnable battle.

Breaking the binge isn't easy. Our phones are programmed to follow us around, distract us from everything else and make us feel good about being kidnapped from life. In fact, the world's brightest minds are priming us to fall in love with our kidnappers. When I say goodbye to Siri, she doesn't say goodbye to me. She replies with a breezy but stalkerish, 'See you later'. In some ways, by listening to every conversation, mapping my taps and noting down my locations in real time, my device *is* stalking me. And in a dystopian twist, when I am away from my stalker and separated from my phone, I feel unsteady, even unsafe. We're all experiencing some sort of Stockholm syndrome but here are some strategies for breaking up with your kidnapper:

1) **Move your butt:** Just as on-screen sirens have gone from voluptuous to size zero, our phones have transformed from heavy devices to sleek, skinny tools that effortlessly glide into everything. As they move back and forth from our purses and pockets to our hands, it becomes evident that the portability, the *everywhereness* of phones make them the perfect delivery vehicles for addictive content. Research suggests that 75 per cent of us can always reach our phones without moving our feet. Can you do it right now—reach your phone without moving your feet? If so, it's time to literally move your butt.

2) **Bring out the shoebox:** It's our family movie night, but I've been on my phone through half the movie. I look up and notice that Darshan is on his phone too. Then I look over to Zoya and wonder what she's thinking as both her parents tap away, their numb faces lit up by these solo screens instead of looking at the big screen on which we're all supposed to watch a movie together. Speaking of solo, we were watching *Free Solo* that night, a documentary about mountaineer Alex Honnold's rope-free climb of El Capitan, a formidable vertical rock. Honnold lets go of the rope and attempts to climb the mountain. Resolving to make a tech-related change in our family, I take the rope off my neck and attempt to climb my own mountain. Soon phone-free dinners follow which include a family-wide rule with no exceptions including the adults. It takes some getting used to and at first, we have an actual box into which we deposit our phones before sitting down at the table. It's rudimentary but surprisingly effective. A few weeks later, we're ready to go phone free with others and form a 'tech bubble' with another similarly-minded family. The rule is simple: whoever violates the rules by checking their phone pays for dinner!

3) **Tune into yourself:** Zoya asks me for an Apple Watch for her eleventh birthday, and I ask her why she wants it. 'Convince me,' I suggest. She takes a deep breath as she prepares for what she clearly considers an annoying uphill task. 'Three reasons. One, so I can see how many steps I've done; two, to see how much I've slept; and three, so that I don't miss

anything,' she replies. Technology has convinced iGen that every aspect of their waking (and sleeping) lives must be monitored, recorded and analysed.

Imagine walking into a room and meeting a person you've never met before. Within seconds of meeting you, they tell you that you had a spicy jalapeño pizza with extra cheese for lunch, that you called your mother from the car after which you had a passive-aggressive email exchange with your boss. Two hours ago, you sent a flirty text to someone who wasn't your spouse, who sent a screenshot of it to a WhatsApp group, which then laughed at you. This person knows which of your college friends you keep in touch with, how much you hate your job, every one of your 'get rich quick' ideas and your secret sexual fantasy, yes, the one that you haven't told anyone. This is what a few hours of data collection would look like for an ordinary person. Many of us are leaking all of that data and much more in exchange for an app that informs us how many steps we've taken and when it's time to go to bed. This data is clearly a gold mine for Big Tech—a gift tied up with a giant bow but it's worth considering if Tech's paltry return gift to you is worth it. An alternative might be to tap into our own circadian rhythms to figure out what generations before us have effortlessly estimated—bedtime. And as our kids watch us model a purposeful use of tech, they'll hopefully have better ideas for birthday presents.

4)   **Go grey:** Rishi is a successful hedge fund manager with a job that often requires an early morning

start. Despite setting an alarm for 6 a.m., Rishi says he stays awake for hours into the night watching deep-state videos on military policy. 'It's compulsive watching. I know I'll barely get any sleep, but I can't stop watching it. My phone just lines up the next video,' he says resignedly. Perhaps we need to worry less about limiting our kids' screen time and more about limiting our own. Technology recognizes no boundaries and so, creating as well as patrolling these lines of control is on us. There are some easy ways to get started. The 'Do Not Disturb' feature ensures that you are not interrupted by every WhatsApp forward and property broker, but only when an important call comes in. Permanently disable all social media notifications and make a habit of placing your phone face down on tables. Then there's the matter of going grey! Much like our primate cousins, humans have primitive minds that are easily stimulated by bright colours (we haven't evolved all that much). This partially explains why you pick the brightly coloured box of laundry detergent over the black-and-white dancing girl at the grocery store. Silicon Valley companies like Facebook and Google know this and are increasingly turning to neuroscience to learn more about how our brains respond to colour in apps, what brings pleasure and what grabs our attention.[4] Consider turning your phone to greyscale and removing colour from the home screen. Regardless of what your hairstylist says, it may be time to go grey.

CHAPTER NINE

GOLDILOCKS

I am en route to Delhi and instead of the gentle namaste of the air hostess, I am greeted with a punch on the arm and a loud squeal. Tanvi is a childhood friend: someone I've known my entire life. Of late our conversations have become thin and brittle; we communicate through quick emojis dropped on each other's Instagram posts. But here, with our phones on airplane mode, there is an opportunity to really connect. Our seats are quickly swapped with a gentleman who can't wait to get out of the way; he clearly doesn't want to be stuck in between long-lost school buddies especially ones who squeal. We buckle up and settle down to swap stories. Tanvi is an educator who recently visited an innovative IB school in Bengaluru that works with cutting-edge technology. She tells me all about it. 'The kids' assessments are all done by AI. When a student answers a question on a test, AI marks the answer and suggests how the kid could have responded differently. They have an Oculus available for every four kids!' she relays excitedly. The rest of the plane ride comprises electrifying thoughts about how she plans to incorporate this technology in the schools that she runs in Delhi. 'What do you think?' she asks, as the plane descends and laudably penetrates Delhi's polluted winter veil. 'Well, the future *is* coming,' I respond.

Our children may not be taught by robots (yet), but the twenty-first century will be dominated by new technology arriving at breakneck speeds including AI and biotechnology. As we collect our luggage, Tanvi continues to insist that we must learn to thrive with technology. She's right, of course, but my mind—unlike Delhi's pollution—has drifted in a different direction. As parents, how do we mitigate the problems that will come with adopting the high-speed technology that is hurtling down the highway? What kind of seatbelts should we use for our children? Can we just stare out of the car window? Is blissful ignorance an option here? The Romans suggested that when an ostrich sensed danger, it immediately buried its head in the sand voluntarily blinding itself to the approaching threat.* 'If I can't see the problem, perhaps the problem can't see me,' reasoned the ever-optimistic (and somewhat delusional) ostrich. Except, of course, that a clueless ostrich makes for a very enticing target. Giving in to the ubiquitous nature of technology, many of us parents seem to stick our necks in the sand in the hope that the danger will simply pass us by. Unfortunately, all we're doing is making ourselves ostrich-sized targets: the Internet is merciless on those who don't regulate it.

A few days later, I find myself chaperoning my son to yet another birthday party. After we watch the cake being mangled by pre-schoolers hopped up on candy floss, Alia, the birthday boy's mother, and I find a quiet moment to sit down. Listening to *Baby Shark* on loop requires a 2000-calorie refreshment and as we cut into our cake slices, Alia announces that she's decided to give the newly minted five-year-old Jai his very own smartphone as a birthday present. 'He's going to get one eventually. May as well give it to him now,' she responds as my eyebrows soar higher than the party balloons. Jai doesn't respond when I ask him about his phone; he's in Alia's lap but buried beneath the apps. Later, hanging around at the same party, I am introduced to Aditi.

---

* The Romans were wrong. Ostriches are smart.

I pretend not to know who she is during the introduction (I seem to have a pathological need to appear cool even at a preschool birthday party), but the truth is that Aditi's reputation precedes her. She is spearheading a campaign to ban all electronic devices in schools. One of the key points of her agenda is returning to the paper and pens of yore. As you can imagine, her tween daughter is less than thrilled about this. 'You may as well make us use feather quills and ink pots, mom,' Aditi's daughter groans, 'are you *purposely trying* to make me the most unpopular kid in school?'

I have known for a long time that I have my best ideas when I'm hopped up on buttercream fondant and today is no different. As I drive back from the party, I realize that the answer lies neither with Alia nor with Aditi. There's another smart woman who may be able to get us out of this mess—Goldilocks. You might recall how she liked her porridge. Yes, that's it. Not too hot. Not too cold. But just right.

Be Like Goldilocks

Handing your pre-schooler, a smartphone likely means you're a digital enabler: you're going in too hot. Trying to create a 100 per cent screen-free environment slots you as a digital limiter: you're going in too cold. Seeing that she likes things just right, Goldilocks is a digital mentor who explores online spaces with her kids and allows them to come to her with questions so they can have the healthiest, safest digital experiences possible.

If Goldilocks were here, she'd remind us that the secret to the perfect porridge is to keep monitoring its temperature and adjusting things as you go along.

Remember when you watched your baby like a hawk and accompanied them everywhere? Those eagle-eyed years passed and you began to let them go to some places unaccompanied (you needed to conserve your sanity to survive the class birthday parties anyway). As they grew up, you learned how to back off: the porridge needed a dollop of independence. Soon you were there just for drop-offs and pick-ups before realizing that it was time for your child to learn how to drive on their own. The porridge needed yet another spoon of independence. A heaped spoonful this time. So, literally and metaphorically, you gave your kid the driver's seat. But here's the thing: your kid didn't learn how to drive overnight. It took endless hours of supervision and practice before you granted them that privilege.

I'll be the first to admit that perfecting the porridge is not going to be easy. It doesn't matter if you're a trained Cordon Bleu chef—technology management will often be the most testing recipe of any parent's life. Not too hot, not too cold. It's a recipe that can quickly ruin if you don't stir it at the right time. Constant physical supervision, particularly as they enter adolescence, will quickly result in burnt porridge (and resentful kids). Conversely, a completely laissez-faire approach would be equivalent to serving stone-cold porridge. But the good news is that you don't have to stir the pot forever—after all, we are raising adults, not twenty-year-old toddlers who require constant monitoring. Once the kids have internalized the lesson on regulating technology, we won't—and shouldn't be—physically present to supervise every keystroke. A German proverb suggests that a parent should give their child two things: roots and wings. That's exactly what it means to be a digital Goldilocks.

Giving them a Fiat before the Ferrari

What you and I will forever refer to as 'digital Goldilocks', others call the *slow tech* movement. It's a quiet movement that is tricky to spot because influencers tend to use louder megaphones. But it exists, and it is followed by the biggest names in technology. Bill Gates didn't give his children smartphones until they turned fourteen[1] and when Steve Jobs released the first iPad, he didn't allow his kid to use it.[2] 'We limit how much technology our kids use at home,' Jobs said. Few people have understood modern technology better than Gates and Jobs, *and it is because of this understanding, not despite it*, that their parenting style is low tech, slow tech. It might be worth taking a page from their book: go low and slow. And just to be clear, slow tech doesn't mean no tech. It simply advocates an approach where technology is moderated so that it is part of the fabric of life and not life itself.

Each of us will interpret this differently; one parent in my slow tech group says that she has given her ten-year-old son a phone to text family and friends, but she must be informed before he adds any new contacts. Another says that her fourteen-year-old daughter has had a phone for two years with all passwords known to immediate family members. The passwords can only be made private after six months of consistent school performance. A third parent in the group puts it quite simply, 'My eleven-year-old has a phone, but it isn't a smartphone. He gets a Fiat before we give him the Ferrari.'

Regardless of whether you hand your kid the keys to a Fiat or a Ferrari, you are the authority that stamps the driving licence. This is a great opportunity to come up with a contract that works for everyone. Begin with a family mission statement and be as specific as possible. Think about the values—kindness, transparency, authenticity—that are important to your family. The central question here is *what do we live by as family?* Each of us must do online as we would do offline and so an honest answer to this question is key.* Once everyone in the family has agreed on the mission statement, here are a few other talking points:

- Be open and honest with me. We all make mistakes IRL, so it's likely that errors will be made online too. Things will happen, and, whether it's a leaked nude photo or a social media post gone wrong, I would like to know sooner rather than later. I am more likely to be accommodating if you are honest with me. Besides, we are better positioned to help you damage control before things completely tailspin. In return for your honesty, I promise to stand in your corner and not shame you.

- While I don't expect perfection, I do expect you to learn from your mistakes. If you're willing to do that, then we don't necessarily need to scale back your access to technology. When you demonstrate that you can learn from your mistakes, I can take an 'assist, not restrict' approach when something negative happens.

---

* But the flip side of this coin shines just as brightly; as we ask our children to live by our family values, we, as parents, must do the same. So, if your family value is authenticity then that old lament about '*Log kya kahenge?*' needs to die because if all that matters is your neighbour's opinion, you should be fine with your kid having a Finsta account. The neighbours will never know!

- I know that you have the option to lie to me about where you are, but I also have the option to geolocate you on apps like 360Live and place AirTags on your bags. Let's make smart choices here.

- Not all Apples grow on trees. Don't expect me to replace the phone if you lose or damage it. You should also know that a new phone drop doesn't necessarily mean it's going to drop into our family. In fact, old or new, this phone isn't a gift to you. It remains family property and as a result, sharing passwords will be an evolving conversation.

- We are all dealing with the fallout of addiction at various levels. It's safe to say that we are experiencing a tech pandemic at a global scale. And just like Covid, some of us will be hit harder than others but no-one will remain unaffected. As a parent, my brain feels broken by technology sometimes, but I am determined to use what I've learned to keep your brain from breaking too. In the words of the immortal Jerry Maguire, 'Help me help you'.

Good luck, Goldilocks. Now back to stirring the porridge.

Epilogue

As this book draws to a close, I have an epiphany that shakes me to the core. This book would not have been possible without the Internet. But wait, that's not the epiphany—I have already acknowledged the majesty of the Internet in a previous chapter hailing it as a critical resource, an updated dictionary (that helpfully includes iGen slang), an inexhaustible thesaurus, an efficient research assistant and an assiduous fact-checker all in one. But here's where the penny drops: as I learn from the Internet and weave it into a narrative for you, could it be that the final product—my beloved book—is, in fact, not solely my work? Is this book the output of a human–machine hybrid? Should the credits read 'Neha plus Internet' in big, bold letters on the front cover? And if I have, in fact, co-authored this book with Google, then surely it won't be long before ChatGPT and Google join hands and exclude me from the team. Google could do the fact-checking while ChatGPT makes quick work of the prose. The probability of likely obsoletion makes the world shift from underneath my feet.

It's worth remembering that ChatGPT is just the tip of the iceberg and by the time you hold this book in your hands, there will be countless more AI applications with all manners of real-world implications. If ChatGPT can pose a threat to the livelihood of authors and DALL ·E 2 can put artists out of business, it's only a matter of time before the contours of every job change. We now live in a different world, one that evolves by the minute and plays by its own rules. It's difficult to predict which way things will go and what any of this really means. Luckily, some things will remain true through the ages: chocolate will always be the best flavour of ice cream, and wisdom will always lie in knowing that we do not know. Or at the very least knowing that (sometimes) the kids know better. YouTuber, gamer and influencer have replaced yesterday's doctor, lawyer and engineer and so, we watch dumbstruck as our kids rise to the top of professions that we mistakenly still think of as 'hobbies'.

Kids today are solving problems both new and ancient. As I write this, a student at the University of Cambridge has solved a Sanskrit grammar conundrum that had puzzled scholars across the world for thousands of years. Rishi Rajpopat had spent months agonizing over the problem and was 'getting nowhere' when he decided to take a break.* He spent the summer swimming, cycling, cooking and meditating before returning to his books.

---

* Head back to Chapter 5 to learn more about how the Dutch, amongst the happiest people in the world, endorse the idea of taking a break and 'doing nothing' to boost creativity.

It turns out that stepping back helped him take a giant step forward; 'within minutes, as I turned the pages, these patterns started emerging, and it all started to make sense,' he says. Rishi's eureka moment highlights the importance of putting in the work but pausing to take a breath. I read about Rishi and think back to Goldilocks—not too hot, not too cold but just right. Getting the temperature of the porridge to be perfect seems crucial in our oversaturated, tech-driven lives. Over the years, we have fed ourselves endless myths about productivity and complicated our lives with noise and notifications in an attempt to stay hyper-productive. It's almost as if we measure our self-worth by how much we produce, by the efficiency of our output. Think about what else gets measured like that— machines. And as more of our work shifts to human-machine hybrids, we have to remember that *we are the human part of that partnership.*

As we strive to conserve our humanity, we must know that it is not technology that is depleting our intimacy with ourselves and others. Instead, it is our inability to *balance* technology that causes this deficit. The Internet gives us the illusion of both fame and anonymity—such magnetic, powerful draws. From news to nudes, everything is always available online and that's enticing too. But how much we give in to that seduction is finally up to us and if we wait for Big Tech to regulate our consumption for us, then we'll be waiting forever.

But speaking of balance, we must give credit where it's due; even Big Tech's products can be instruments of catalytic positive change. One of the hallmarks of iGen is how deeply they care about the issues that plague the world. From making Facebook groups that help migrant workers to coordinating oxygen cylinders on Instagram, this is the generation that used social media to show up. In fact, they showed up in the face of the worst global emergency in living memory. They showed up to demonstrate that we didn't need to be paralysed. Far from being unresponsive, they made kindness trend and it was an honour to watch them in action. From their Covid response to the Black Lives Matter and MeToo movements, time and again iGen has used the Internet to galvanize the globe into action. Malala Yousafzai and Greta Thunberg are examples of what you can get done when you hold that megaphone the right way.

iGen is born at a time when the very planet that we live on is at risk. *Maybe that's what gives them this urgent voice that won't be muzzled.* They have watched generations before them senselessly fight over opium and blood diamonds. *Maybe that's why they use their megaphones to ask for change.* They live in a borderless Internet that recognizes no boundaries and yet they watch kings and presidents drop bombs for inches of land. *Maybe that's why they won't stop marching and protesting. Maybe evolution is marching with them. Maybe the Gods are applauding as they protest.* We keep thinking that their phones have softened, even coddled iGen. But watch them in action and it's clear that they're tough enough to change the world. Maybe it's time to stop putting up firewalls and figure out how to join their party. Perhaps the party will be at the neighbour's house or maybe it will be next to Snoop's in the metaverse. Either way, they look like they're having a good time.

Acknowledgements

My first debt of gratitude remains to my parents, Pinku and Pradeep Jhalani. Not readers themselves, they ignited a surprising love for books that continues to burn. It is but one of countless gifts. I am because you are.

No conversation about parents is complete without Kamal and Niranjan Hiranandani. From babysitting the kids when I was away to being unfailing supporters of my work, I am so grateful to have you in my life.

Darshan Hiranandani, who first had the idea for this book and without whom this book wouldn't exist. As I said countless times when I was in the despairing depths of unending revisions, *'This is all your fault!'* It *is* your fault, but it is also your doing.

Kanishka Gupta, agent extraordinaire, who is half-coach and half-sherpa but all heart. Thank you for seeing me through every episode of writer's block and constantly reminding me that this is a book that deserves to be written.

Shantanu Duttagupta whose persuasive perspective on the bright side of tech brought some much-needed

balance to the manuscript. Our friendship may have
arrived late, but I know it stays until the end.

I couldn't have asked for a better set of gurus and
guides than the incredible folks at Penguin Random House
India. Manasi Subramaniam who championed this book
from the start and whose insights have made it sharper,
clearer, stronger. Shreya Punj whose detailed thoughts on
those early drafts made the later drafts that much better.
Shubhi Surana whose keen marketing sense ensures that
this book doesn't just stay on dusty bookshelves. Yash
Daiv and his fine-toothed comb that weeded out so many
errors. Any that remain are on me.

My forum mates both in Mumbai and Dubai, thank
you for patiently listening to me give you updates about
finishing my edits without even once rolling your eyes.
I'm lucky to have you in my corner.

Alisha Patel who is ever ready to brainstorm ideas.
Savitar Jagtiani, tech enthusiast who will always take the
time to share notes, articles, photos, anything that might
help. Ankur Shah who showed up with a torch when the
world went dark one day.

Raghav Katyal who helped me explore my own limits
and pushed me over the finish line. Eventually, everything
that I script comes back covered with your red marks and
I wouldn't have it any other way.

And finally, Zoya and Jahan, for giving me both the
reason and the space to write this book. Thank you for
every time you softly closed the door when I was working,
for every time you quietly settled down when I motioned
that I was on the phone and for every time you crept into
bed beside me, knowing, just knowing that I needed to

sleep in. You two have the biggest hearts in the world and I couldn't be prouder.

And dear reader, how do I acknowledge you? In a new-age world whirling with pings, beeps and sexy Instagram photos, thank you for doing the old-school thing and picking up this book. Knowing that you're out there makes me feel less alone.

Notes

Introduction

1. *Financial Times*, 'Prospering in the Pandemic: The Top 100 Companies', www.ft.com, *Financial Times*, June 19, 2020, https://www.ft.com/content/844ed28c-8074-4856-bde0-20f3bf4cd8f0, accessed on July 5, 2023.
2. Cooper, Anderson, 'Screen Time Kids Study: Groundbreaking Study Examines Effects of Screen Time on Kids—60 Minutes', cbsnews.com, December 10, 2018, https://www.cbsnews.com/news/groundbreaking-study-examines-effects-of-screen-time-on-kids-60-minutes/.
3. Richtel, Matt, 'Children's Screen Time Has Soared in the Pandemic, Alarming Parents and Researchers', *New York Times*, January 16, 2021, sec. Health, https://www.nytimes.com/2021/01/16/health/covid-kids-tech-use.html.

Chapter One

1. Wagner, Kurt, and David McLaughlin, 'Facebook, Alarmed by Teen Usage Drop, Left Investors in the Dark', Bloomberg.com, October 25, 2021, https://www.bloomberg.com/news/articles/2021-10-25/facebook-files-show-growth-struggles-as-young-users-in-u-s-decline.

2. Mehrotra, Kartikay, '17-Year-Old Florida High School Boy Orchestrated Twitter Hack Attack on Obama, Musk, Bezos', the *Print*, August 1, 2020, https://theprint.in/tech/17-year-old-florida-high-school-boy-orchestrated-twitter-hack-attack-on-obama-musk-bezos/472614/.

3. Robertson, Jordan, and Monica Raymunt, 'Teen Cyber Prodigy Stumbled Onto Flaw Letting Him Hijack Teslas', *Bloomberg*, January 13, 2022, https://www.bloomberg.com/news/articles/2022-01-13/german-teen-stumbled-across-flaw-allowing-him-to-hijack-teslas.

4. Company, Facebook, and *Meta*, 'Founder's Letter, 2021', Meta, October 29, 2021, https://about.fb.com/news/2021/10/founders-letter/.

5. Basu, Tanya, 'The Metaverse Has a Groping Problem Already', *MIT Technology Review*, February 4, 2022, https://www.technologyreview.com/2021/12/16/1042516/the-metaverse-has-a-groping-problem/.

6. Das, Amrita, 'Woman Recalls "Gang Rape" in Metaverse; Concerns Grow over Making VR Platforms Safe from Sexual Predators', cnbctv18.com, February 8, 2022. https://www.cnbctv18.com/technology/woman-recalls-gang-rape-in-metaverse-concerns-grow-over-making-vr-platforms-safe-from-sexual-predators-12396992.htm.

Chapter Two

1. Media and Public Relations | Baylor University, 'Cellphone Addiction Is "an Increasingly Realistic Possibility", Baylor Study of College Students Reveals', n.d. https://www.baylor.edu/mediacommunications/news.php?action=story&story=145864. 4

2. Parkin, Simon, 'Has Dopamine Got Us Hooked on Tech?' *Guardian*, March 21, 2018, https://www.theguardian.com/technology/2018/mar/04/has-dopamine-got-us-hooked-on-tech-facebook-apps-addiction.

3. Bastone, Nick, 'Snapchat Founder Evan Spiegel and Wife Miranda Kerr Limit Their Seven-Year-Old Child to 1.5 Hours of Screen Time per Week', *Business Insider*, December 31, 2018, https://www.businessinsider.com/evan-spiegel-miranda-kerr-screen-time-2018-12.

4. Paige, Danielle, 'What Happens in Your Brain When You Binge-Watch a TV Show,' NBC News November 4, 2017, https://www.nbcnews.com/better/health/what-happens-your-brain-when-you-binge-watch-tv-series-ncna816991.

5. Snider, Mike, 'Netflix's Biggest Competition? Sleep, CEO Says', *USA TODAY*, April 18, 2017, https://www.usatoday.com/story/tech/talkingtech/2017/04/18/netflixs-biggest-competition-sleep-ceo-says/100585788/.

6. Parkin, Simon, 'Has Dopamine Got Us Hooked on Tech?' *Guardian*, March 21, 2018, https://www.theguardian.com/technology/2018/mar/04/has-dopamine-got-us-hooked-on-tech-facebook-apps-addiction.

7. Harris, Tristan, 'How a Handful of Tech Companies Control Billions of Minds Every Day', Ted Talks, https://www.ted.com/talks/tristan_harris_how_a_handful_

of_tech_companies_control_billions_of_minds_every_day?language=en.

8. BBC News, 'AI "godfather" Geoffrey Hinton Tells the BBC of AI Dangers after He Quits Google', BBC May 2, 2001, https://www.bbc.com/news/av/world-us-canada-65453192.

9. @yuval_noah_harari Instagram post, July 22, 2021.

10. Clark, Kaitlin, 'The 7 Biggest Plastic Surgery Trends of 2022 | Plastic Surgeons Predict the Most Popular Procedures', *Allure*, January 16, 2022, https://www.allure.com/story/plastic-surgery-trends-2022.

11. Criddle, Cristina, 'Body-Editing Apps on TikTok "Trigger Eating Disorders"', BBC News, March 27, 2021, https://www.bbc.com/news/technology-56503546.

12. Conversation, Jean Twenge, 'Teen Suicide Rates Are Higher among Girls – and It Has to Do with How They Use Social Media', Scroll.in, January 19, 2020, https://scroll.in/article/950220/teen-suicide-rates-are-higher-among-girls-and-it-has-to-do-with-how-they-use-social-media.

13. Wells, Georgia, Jeff Horwitz, and Deepa Seetharaman, 'Facebook Knows Instagram Is Toxic for Teen Girls, Company Documents Show', *Wall Street Journal*, September 14, 2021, https://www.wsj.com/articles/facebook-knows-instagram-is-toxic-for-teen-girls-company-documents-show-11631620739.

14. Royal Society for Public Health, 'Instagram Ranked Worst for Young People's Mental Health', https://www.rsph.org.uk/about-us/news/instagram-ranked-worst-for-young-people-s-mental-health.html.

15. Shah, Shivanshi, 'India's Gen Z, Who Love the "GRAM"', YouGov, May 25, 2023 https://business.

yougov.com/content/8256-profile-peek-india-gen-z-who-love-the-gram?utm_medium=advertising&utm_source=Afaqs&utm_campaign=ADV-2023-05-IN-Afaqs-Gen-Z-Profile-Peek.

16. Satariano, Adam, 'British Ruling Pins Blame on Social Media for Teenager's Suicide', *New York Times*, October 1, 2022, https://www.nytimes.com/2022/10/01/business/instagram-suicide-ruling-britain.html.

17. Katz, Emily Tess, 'Study Shows 1 In 4 Kids Have Dieted By Age 7', *HuffPost*, March 1, 2017, https://www.huffpost.com/entry/most-10-year-olds-have-been-on-a-diet_n_6532632?ir=India&adsSiteOverride=in.

18. Jones, Harrison, 'Doctor Warns Innocent People Will Die If They Do the "Coronavirus Challenge"', *Metro*, March 24, 2020, https://metro.co.uk/2020/03/24/doctor-warns-innocent-people-will-die-coronavirus-challenge__trashed-12450472/?ito=cbshare.

19. Bogost, Ian, 'The Age of Social Media Is Ending', *The Atlantic*, March 10, 2023, https://www.theatlantic.com/technology/archive/2022/11/twitter-facebook-social-media-decline/672074/.

20. McCluskey, Megan, 'Elon Musk Wants to Rid Twitter of "Spam Bots", Nearly Half His Followers Are Fake', *Time*, April 28, 2022, https://time.com/6171726/elon-musk-fake-followers/.

21. Rose, Frank, 'The Selfish Meme', *The Atlantic*, February 19, 2014, https://www.theatlantic.com/magazine/archive/2012/10/the-selfish-meme/309080/.

22. Twenge, Jean M., 'Have Smartphones Destroyed a Generation?' *The Atlantic*, July 8, 2022, https://www.theatlantic.com/magazine/archive/2017/09/has-the-smartphone-destroyed-a-generation/534198/.

23. @Mojorojo, Instagram, November 16, 2022

24. PTI, 'Indian Teenagers Show Risky Behaviour Online: McAfee', *Mint*, November 10, 2014. https://www.livemint. com/Industry/t7jUP4dxW2P9r9lCDNANHP/Indian-teenagers-show-risky-behaviour-online-McAfee.html.

25. Twenge, Jean M, et al., 'Worldwide Increases in Adolescent Loneliness', *Journal of Adolescence* 93, no. 1 (December 1, 2021): 257–69. https://doi.org/10.1016/j. adolescence.2021.06.006.

26. Twenge, Jean M., Brian H. Spitzberg, and W. Keith Campbell, 'Less In-Person Social Interaction with Peers among U.S. Adolescents in the 21st Century and Links to Loneliness', *Journal of Social and Personal Relationships* 36, no. 6 (March 19, 2019): 1892–1913. https://doi. org/10.1177/0265407519836170.

27. Pew Research Center: Internet, Science & Tech, 'Teens, Technology and Friendships | Pew Research Center', May 30, 2020, https://www.pewresearch.org/internet/ 2015/08/06/teens-technology-and-friendships/.

28. Anon., 'Teen Mental Health Deep Dive', *Wall Street Journal*, n,d., https://s.wsj.net/public/resources/documents/ teen-mental-health-deep-dive.pdf.

29. Kaplan News, 'Kaplan Survey: College Admissions Officers Increasingly Say Applicants' Social Media Content is "Fair Game"', Kaplan Blog, January 28, 2024, https://www.kaptest.com/blog/press/2021/01/28/kaplan-survey-college-admissions-officers-increasingly-say-applicants-social-media-content-is-fair-game/.

30. Twenge, Jean M., and Gabrielle N. Martin., 'Gender Differences in Associations between Digital Media Use and Psychological Well-being: Evidence from Three Large Datasets', Journal of Adolescence 79, no. 1

(January 8, 2020): 91–102, https://doi.org/10.1016/j. adolescence.2019.12.018.

31. Ghorayshi, Azeen, and Roni Caryn Rabin, 'Teen Girls Report Record Levels of Sadness, CDC Finds', *New York Times*, May 10, 2023, https://www.nytimes.com/2023/02/13/health/teen-girls-sadness-suicide-violence.html.

32. Leighton, Heather, 'Influencers Admit That Instagram Is Bad For Body Image, Mental Health, Study Shows', *Forbes*, December 14, 2019, https://www.forbes.com/sites/heatherleighton/2019/12/13/is-instagram-bad-for-your-mental-health-body-image/.

33. Goldman, Jeremy, 'Analyst Take: Is BeReal for Real?' *Insider Intelligence*, October 19, 2022, https://www.insiderintelligence.com/content/analyst-take-bereal-real.

34. Bogost, Ian, 'The Age of Social Media Is Ending', *The Atlantic*, March 10, 2023, https://www.theatlantic.com/technology/archive/2022/11/twitter-facebook-social-media-decline/672074/.

35. Steyer, James P. *Talking Back to Facebook: The Common Sense Guide to Raising Kids in the Digital Age*. Scribner, 2012, P. 45.

36. Hunt, Melissa, Rachel Marx, Courtney Lipson, and Jordyn Young, 'No More FOMO: Limiting Social Media Decreases Loneliness and Depression', *Journal of Social and Clinical Psychology* 37, no. 10 (December 1, 2018): 751–68. https://doi.org/10.1521/jscp.2018.37.10.751.

37. Wetsman, Nicole, 'Facebook Isn't Telling the Whole Story about Its Mental Health Research', *The Verge*, October 28, 2021, https://www.theverge.com/2021/10/28/22749357/facebook-mental-health-research-tobacco.

38.   Ginsberg, David, and Moira Burke, 'Hard Questions: Is Spending Time on Social Media Bad for Us?', About Facebook, December 15, 2017. https://about.fb.com/news/2017/12/hard-questions-is-spending-time-on-social-media-bad-for-us/.

Chapter Three

1.   Uniyal, Ruchika, 'Majority of Indian Women Sext, Many Use Apps to Find Partners', *The Times of India*, September 18, 2020, https://timesofindia.indiatimes.com/india/majority-of-indian-women-sext-many-use-apps-to-find-partners/articleshow/78186218.cms.

2.   Doble, Anna, 'UK's Fastest Growing Language Is... Emoji', BBC News, May 19, 2015. http://www.bbc.co.uk/newsbeat/article/32793732/uks-fastest-growing-language-is-emoji.

3.   Gallagher, Billy, 'How Reggie Brown Invented Snapchat', TechCrunch, February 10, 2018. http://tcrn.ch/2CcfdVU.

4.   'Social Media, SRE, and Sensible Drinking: Understanding the Dramatic Decline in Teenage Pregnancy', British Pregnancy Advisory Service, https://www.bpas.org/media/3037/bpas-teenage-pregnancy-report.pdf.

5.   Horne, Marc, 'Sexting Rise May Help to Lower Teen Pregnancy Rate', *The Times*, July 5, 2023, sec. Scotland, https://www.thetimes.co.uk/article/sexting-rise-may-help-to-lower-teen-pregnancy-rate-9mt62s6dt.

6.   Smith, Brendan, 'Are Internet Affairs Different?', APA, *Https://Www.Apa.Org*, d. https://www.apa.org/monitor/2011/03/internet.

7.   Ibid.

8.   Wikipedia contributors, 'Second Life', Wikipedia, June 28, 2023, https://en.wikipedia.org/wiki/Second_Life.

9. Anderer, John, 'Love in the Age of Lockdown: 63% of Americans Say Dating Will Never Be the Same Again', *Study Finds*, November 12, 2020. https://studyfinds.org/lockdown-love-dating-never-be-same-again/.

10. https://www.lovetreats.in/products/we-vibe-jive?variant=28352123764841

11. Kannan, Saikiran, 'Pornography Gets a Pandemic Boost, India Reports 95 per cent Rise in Viewing', *India Today*, April 11, 2020. https://www.indiatoday.in/news-analysis/story/pornography-gets-a-pandemic-boost-india-reports-95-per-cent-rise-in-viewing-1665940-2020-04-11.

12. Steyer, *Talking Back to Facebook*, 69.

13. TNN, 'Survey: 70% of Boys Began Watching Porn at 10 Years', Coimbatore News, The Times of India, July 25, 2015, https://timesofindia.indiatimes.com/city/coimbatore/survey-70-of-boys-began-watching-porn-at-10-years/articleshow/48209402.cms.

14. Biggs, John, 'Researchers Find That Filters Don't Prevent Porn', TechCrunch, July 13, 2018, https://techcrunch.com/2018/07/13/researchers-find-that-filters-dont-prevent-porn/.

15. Price Chris, 'Escenic', *The Telegraph*, https://www.telegraph.co.uk/women/sex/6709646/All-men-watch-porn-scientists-find.html.

16. Koletić, Goran, 'Longitudinal Associations between the Use of Sexually Explicit Material and Adolescents' Attitudes and Behaviors: A Narrative Review of Studies', *Journal of Adolescence* 57, no. 1 (April 20, 2017): 119–33, https://doi.org/10.1016/j.adolescence.2017.04.006.

17. McNamara, Brittney, 'Can Porn Help People Understand Consent?' *Teen Vogue*, April 30, 2019, https://www.teenvogue.com/story/can-porn-make-consent-sexy.

18. Steiner–Adair, Catherine, and Teresa Barker. 2013. *The Big Disconnect: Protecting Childhood and Family Relationships in the Digital Age.* Harper Collins.

19. Code Computerlove, 'Students Turn to Porn to Fill the Gaps in Their Sex Education', Nus.org.uk, 2015, https://www.nus.org.uk/en/news/students-turn-to-porn-to-fill-the-gaps-in-their-sex-education/.

20. 'Young Hongkongers Are Watching More Porn, but Know Less about Sex', South China Morning Post, June 12, 2017, https://www.scmp.com/news/hong-kong/health-environment/article/2097985/worrying-rise-hong-kong-pupils-watching-porn-their.

21. Wood Rocket, "Ask A Porn Star: "Real Sex VS Porn Sex"", April 6, 2016, https://www.youtube.com/watch?v=RDwsFVH-ZLc.

22. Ibid

23. Robertevans, 'Headline', *Cracked*, June 29, 2014, https://www.cracked.com/personal-experiences-1386-5-reasons-being-male-porn-star-less-fun-than-it-looks.html.

24. '4 Surprising Downsides to Being a Porn Star - Cracked Goes There with Robert Evans', www.youtube.com, July 5, 2023, https://www.youtube.com/watch?v=vQxu87Y9gLU.

25. Glass, Jeremy, 'Male Porn Stars Share Their Secrets for Staying Hard on Set', *Men's Health*, November 2, 2021, https://www.menshealth.com/sex-women/a19546917/porn-stars-share-how-they-stay-hard-on-set/.

26. Kbcreativelab, 'Porn Sex vs Real Sex: The Differences Explained With Food', July 29, 2013, https://www.youtube.com/watch?v=q64hTNEj6KQ.

27. https://www.tiktok.com/@kleblanc123/video/6842025121431997702

28. Moore, Anna, and Coco Khan, 'The Fatal, Hateful Rise of Choking during Sex', *Guardian*, July 25, 2019, https://www.theguardian.com/society/2019/jul/25/fatal-hateful-rise-of-choking-during-sex.

29. Fry, Ellie, 'TikTok, Netflix's "365 Days" and the Memeification of Violent Sex by Generation Z', *Independent*, August 26, 2020, https://www.independent.co.uk/life-style/women/tiktok-365-days-netflix-rough-sex-defence-film-domestic-abuse-a9677051.html.

30. Richardson, Hannah, 'Warn Children about Porn Earlier, Teens Say', BBC News, December 16, 2021, https://www.bbc.com/news/education-59666170.

31. Kalra, Shreya, 'Violent Rape Pornography Is Turning Indian Men On, We Tell You What's Going Wrong', *IndiaTimes*, March 8, 2017, https://www.indiatimes.com/news/india/rape-pornography-is-turning-indian-men-on-we-tell-you-what-s-going-wrong-with-this-268734.html.

32. TNN, '40% Goan Youth Watch Rape Porn, Finds Survey', *Times of India*, July 25, 2014, https://timesofindia.indiatimes.com/city/goa/40-goan-youth-watch-rape-porn-finds-survey/articleshow/38986007.cms?from=mdr&utm_source=contentofinterest&utm_medium=text&utm_campaign=cppst.

33. Bridges, Ana J., Robert Wosnitzer, Erica Scharrer, Chyng Sun, and Rachael Liberman, 'Aggression and Sexual Behavior in Best-Selling Pornography Videos: A Content Analysis Update', *Violence Against Women* 16, no. 10 (October 1, 2010): 1065–85. https://doi.org/10.1177/1077801210382866.

34. Steiner–Adair and Barker, *The Big Disconnect,* Harper paperback (2014).

35. Brown, Jane D., and Kelly L'Engle, 'X-Rated', *Communication Research* 36, no. 1 (February 1, 2009): 129–51. https://doi.org/10.1177/0093650208326465.

36. Rostad, Whitney L., Daniel Gittins-Stone, Charlie Huntington, Christie J. Rizzo, Deborah N Pearlman, and Lindsay M. Orchowski, 'The Association Between Exposure to Violent Pornography and Teen Dating Violence in Grade 10 High School Students', *Archives of Sexual Behavior* 48, no. 7 (July 15, 2019): 2137–47. https://doi.org/10.1007/s10508-019-1435-4.

37. Harte, Alys, 'A Man Tried to Choke Me during Sex without Warning', BBC News, November 28, 2019, https://www.bbc.com/news/uk-50546184.

38. Steiner–Adair and Barker, *The Big Disconnect*, 186

39. Kharif, Olga, 'Kids Flock to Roblox for Parties and Playdates During Lockdown', *Bloomberg*, April 15, 2020, https://www.bloomberg.com/news/articles/2020-04-15/kids-flock-to-roblox-for-parties-and-playdates-during-lockdown.

40. Dyer, James Clayton & Jasmin, 'Roblox: The Children's Game with a Sex Problem', BBC News, February 15, 2022, https://www.bbc.com/news/technology-60314572.

41. BBC News, 'Warn Children about Porn Earlier, Teens Say', December 16, 2021, sec. Family & Education, https://www.bbc.com/news/education-59666170.

42. 'Online Sports Betting and Casino | BetWinner', n.d., http://lighthouseinsights.in/tweens-teens-and-technology-2014-mcafee-report.html/.

43. Ismail, Shajahan, Ashika Shajahan, Ts Sathyanarayana Rao, and Kevan Wylie, 'Adolescent Sex Education in India: Current Perspectives', *Indian Journal of Psychiatry* 57,

no. 4 (January 1, 2015): 333. https://doi.org/10.4103/0019-5545.171843.

44. Kristof, Nicholas, 'Opinion | The Children of Pornhub', *The New York Times*, December 10, 2020, https://www.nytimes.com/2020/12/04/opinion/sunday/pornhub-rape-trafficking.html?referringSource=articleShare.

45. Brown, Jessica, 'Is Porn Harmful? The Evidence, the Myths and the Unknowns', BBC Future, February 24, 2022, https://www.bbc.com/future/article/20170926-is-porn-harmful-the-evidence-the-myths-and-the-unknowns.

46. Williams, Lee, 'Hooked on Porn, Turned off Sex', *Independent*, August 3, 2016, https://www.independent.co.uk/life-style/health-and-families/hooked-on-porn-turned-off-sex-a7169701.html?r=1056.

47. Manson, Mark, 'How Pornography Can Ruin Your Sex Life', *Mark Manson* (blog), June 23, 2023, https://markmanson.net/pornography-can-ruin-your-sex-life.

Chapter Four

1. Jim Steyer, *Talking Back to Facebook: The Common Sense Guide to Raising Kids in the Digital Age,* Scribner, 2012.

2. UNICEF, 'Child Online Production in India', n.d., https://www.icmec.org/wp-content/uploads/2016/09/UNICEF-Child-Protection-Online-India-pub_doc115-1.pdf

3. McAfee, 'Revenge Posts on Social Media Could Land You in Jail', McAfee Blog, September 3, 2021. https://www.mcafee.com/blogs/mobile-security/revenge-posts-on-social-media-could-land-you-in-jail/.

4. See note 2.

5. Jacobs, Alexandra, 'Book Review: "Monsters: A Fan's Dilemma", by Claire Dederer', *The New York Times*, April 28, 2023, https://www.nytimes.com/2023/04/23/books/monsters-review-claire-dederer.html.

6. Kleinman, Zoe, 'Political Trolling Twice as Popular as Positivity, Study Suggests', BBC News, June 21, 2021, https://www.bbc.com/news/technology-57558028.

7. Abbas, Muntazir, 'India's Growing Data Usage, Smartphone Adoption to Boost Digital India Initiatives: Top Bureaucrat', The Economic Times, October 26, 2021, https://economictimes.indiatimes.com/news/india/indias-growing-data-usage-smartphone-adoption-to-boost-digital-india-initiatives-top-bureaucrat/articleshow/87275402.cms.

8. Sethi, Chitleen K., 'Chandigarh University: SIT Finds "No Objectionable Videos" of Other Women on Phone of Suspect', ThePrint, November 17, 2022, https://theprint.in/india/chandigarh-university-sit-finds-no-objectionable-videos-of-other-women-on-phone-of-suspect/1221855/.

9. Parkin, Simon, 'Has Dopamine Got Us Hooked on Tech?' *Guardian*, March 4, 2018, https://www.theguardian.com/technology/2018/mar/04/has-dopamine-got-us-hooked-on-tech-facebook-apps-addiction.

10. Nagarajan, Shalini., 'Facebook's Stock Price Has Had a Rollercoaster Year Driven by an Ad Boycott, Censorship Controversies, and Blockbuster Results. Here Are Its Biggest Moves in 2020', Markets Insider, July 5, 2023, https://markets.businessinsider.com/news/stocks/facebook-shares-react-badly-ad-boycott-big-stock-moves-2020-7-1029365957.

11. BBC HARDtalk, 'Mia Khalifa: "Porn Is Not Reality"', September 6, 2019, https://www.youtube.com/watch?v=i2qplvJ6SLs.

12. Sarkar, Brinda, 'Local Lawyer Wins Revenge Porn Case', *Telegraph India*, August 24, 2018, https://www.telegraphindia.com/west-bengal/local-lawyer-wins-revenge-porn-case/cid/1412240.

Chapter Five

1. Horowitz, Evan, 'IQ Rates Are Dropping in Many Developed Countries and That Doesn't Bode Well for Humanity', NBC News, May 22, 2019, https://www.nbcnews.com/think/opinion/iq-rates-are-dropping-many-developed-countries-doesn-t-bode-ncna1008576.

2. Catherine Steiner-Adair, *The Big Disconnect: Protecting Childhood and Family Relationships in the Digital Age*, Harper Paperback, 2014.

3. Cooper, Anderson, 'Screen Time Kids Study: Groundbreaking Study Examines Effects of Screen Time on Kids - 60 Minutes', CBS News, December 10, 2018, https://www.cbsnews.com/news/groundbreaking-study-examines-effects-of-screen-time-on-kids-60-minutes/.

4. Turkle, Sherry. *Alone Together: Why We Expect More from Technology and Less from Each Other*, 2017, 163

5. Seppälä, Emma, 'Empathy Is on the Decline in This Country: A New Book Describes What We Can Do to Bring It Back', Washington Post, June 11, 2019, https://www.washingtonpost.com/lifestyle/2019/06/11/empathy-is-decline-this-country-new-book-describes-what-we-can-do-bring-it-back/.

6. Stanford University, 'Heavy Multitaskers Have Reduced Memory', Stanford News, October 25, 2018, https://news.stanford.edu/2018/10/25/decade-data-reveals-heavy-multitaskers-reduced-memory-psychologist-says/.

7. Mollick, Ethan, 'ChatGPT Is a Tipping Point for AI', *Harvard Business Review*, December 14, 2022, https://hbr.org/2022/12/chatgpt-is-a-tipping-point-for-ai.

8. Mecking, Olga, 'The Case for Doing Nothing', *New York Times*, April 30, 2019, https://www.nytimes.com/2019/04/29/smarter-living/the-case-for-doing-nothing.html.

9. Cunff, Anne-Laure Le, 'How to Get in the Flow', *Ness Labs*, May 5, 2020, https://nesslabs.com/flow.

Chapter Six

1. Marcus, Jon, 'Taking a Closer Look at Online Learning in Colleges and Universities', *The New York Times*, October 7, 2022, https://www.nytimes.com/2022/10/06/education/learning/online-learning-higher-education.html.

2. Bhattacharya, Ananya, 'A Teacher Shortage Is Plaguing India's Education System', *Quartz*, July 20, 2022, https://qz.com/india/2182363/india-has-a-shortage-of-school-teachers-both-offline-and-online.

3. Poonam, Snigdha, 'How India Conquered YouTube', *Financial Times*, March 14, 2019, https://www.ft.com/content/c0b08a8e-4527-11e9-b168-96a37d002cd3.

4. Marcus, Jon, 'With Online Learning, "Let's Take a Breath and See What Worked and Didn't Work"', *New York Times*, October 6, 2022, sec. Education. https://www.nytimes.com/2022/10/06/education/learning/online-learning-higher-education.html.

5. Herman, Daniel, 'ChatGPT Will End High-School English', *Atlantic*, December 16, 2022, https://www.theatlantic.com/technology/archive/2022/12/openai-chatgpt-writing-high-school-english-essay/672412/.

6. Milmo, Dan, 'ChatGPT Allowed in International Baccalaureate Essays', *Guardian*, February 27, 2023, https://www.theguardian.com/technology/2023/feb/27/chatgpt-allowed-international-baccalaureate-essays-chatbot

7. Poonam, Snigdha, 'How India Conquered YouTube', *Financial Times*, March 14, 2019, sec. FT Magazine, https://www.ft.com/content/c0b08a8e-4527-11e9-b168-96a37d002cd3.

8. Lilly Singh. "I'll See You Soon...," November 13, 2018, https://www.youtube.com/watch?v=-5OfFk5c01o.

9. @mojorojo, Instagram, November 16, 2022.

10. Anon, '#WhitePaper: Peeking Behind the Influencer Curtain to Mark the 10th Anniversary of Instagram in 2020', n.d., Inzpire, https://blog.inzpire.me/wp-content/uploads/2019/12/inzpireme-Whitepaper.pdf.

11. @mojorojo, Instagram, November 16, 2022.

12. Brooks, Arthur C. 'Parasocial Relationships Are Just Imaginary Friends for Adults'. *Atlantic*, April 6, 2023, https://www.theatlantic.com/family/archive/2023/04/parasocial-relationships-imaginary-connections-fans-celebrities/673645/.

13. 'Instagram Rich List 2021 - Hopper HQ', n.d., www.hopperhq.com, https://www.hopperhq.com/instagram-rich-list/.

14. Kritika Khurana, 'Earning through SOCIAL MEDIA | How Much Do I EARN? 💰 🆘', October 17, 2020, https://www.youtube.com/watch?v=1pu0yyT6m18.

15. Wang, Vivian, 'The Shining Promise and Dashed Dreams of China's Live Shopping Craze', *New York Times*, April 28, 2023, https://www.nytimes.com/2023/04/28/business/china-livestreaming-ecommerce.html?smid=nytcore-ios-share&referringSource=articleShare.

16. Hollander, Jenny, 'Who Are Myka & James Stauffer, Who Face Controversy After "Rehoming" Son Huxley?' *Marie Claire Magazine*, June 26, 2020, https://www.marieclaire. com/culture/a32704035/myka-stauffer-james-rehome-adoption-huxley/

17. 'YouTube Mom Deletes Channel after Criticism of Video with Son Crying', September 14, 2021, https://www. today.com/parents/jordan-cheyenne-speaks-out-about-youtube-video-son-crying-t231055.

18. YouTuber Headlines, 'One of the First Adults Speaking Out about Being Raised on a Mommy Blog + Child Exploitation', January 6, 2021. https://www.youtube. com/watch?v=UebBzm_qjEk.

19. BCCI, Twitter, October 30, 2018, https://twitter.com/bcci/ status/1057136686809972736.

20. tech2 News Staff, 'Indias *PUBG* Mobile Streamer Mortal Talks about That Epic Game, Four-Finger Method', Firstpost, February 1, 2019, https://www.firstpost.com/ tech/gaming/indias-pubg-mobile-streamer-mortal-talks-about-that-epic-game-four-finger-method-6006711. html.

21. Up Gaming, 'Gamer Girls of India | Ep 3: Mysterious YT | Shazia Ayub | First Interview', YouTube June 19, 2019, https://www.youtube.com/watch?v=di_Ajs9kCH8.

22. Nield, David, 'All That Video Gaming Could Be Boosting an Unexpected Life Skill, New Study Finds : ScienceAlert', ScienceAlert, July 15, 2022, https://www.sciencealert. com/all-that-video-gaming-could-be-improving-your-decision-making.

23. Sarkar, Samit, 'Research Shows Playing First-Person Shooters Improves Learning Abilities, Cognitive Function', *Polygon*, January 30, 2013, https://www.polygon.com/

2013/1/30/3932876/research-playing-first-person-shooters-improves-learning-abilities-cognitive-function.

24. Shumaker, Camilla, 'One Hour of Video Gaming Can Increase the Brain's Ability to Focus', University of Arkansas News, February 14, 2018, https://news.uark.edu/articles/40981/one-hour-of-video-gaming-can-increase-the-brain-s-ability-to-focus.

25. 8bit Thug, 'Gaming ,Esports and Money || Thug Talks', June 15, 2021, https://www.youtube.com/watch?v=E15i C8dEeMQ.

26. Ibid

27. 'Edgio Resource Library', n.d., https://www.limelight.com/resources/white-paper/state-of-online-gaming-2019/.

28. News18, '*PUBG* Addiction: Restricted from Playing the Game, 17-Year Old From Haryana Commits Suicide', *News18*, July 8, 2019, https://www.news18.com/news/tech/pubg-addiction-restricted-from-playing-the-game-17-year-old-from-haryana-commits-suicide-2222533.html.

29. NDTV.com, 'Madhya Pradesh Boy, 16, Dies Of Cardiac Arrest While Playing *PUBG*', n.d., https://www.ndtv.com/india-news/madhya-pradesh-boy-16-dies-of-cardiac-arrest-while-playing-online-game-2045675.

30. Siu, William, 'Opinion | I Make Video Games. I Won't Let My Daughters Play Them', *New York Times*, October 2, 2022, https://www.nytimes.com/2022/10/02/opinion/video-game-addiction.html.

31. Lawrence, Kirkland, 'NCSA–Get Recruited. Play Sports in College', *NCSA College Recruiting*, July 3, 2023, https://www.ncsasports.org/college-esports-scholarships/varsity-esports.

32. Team, Dna Web, 'DNA Special: What Is Video Game Addiction? How Serious Is the Problem in India?' *DNA*

India, June 9, 2022, https://www.dnaindia.com/analysis/
report-dna-special-what-is-video-game-addiction-how-
serious-is-the-problem-in-india-2959000.

Chapter Seven

1. Duerager, Andrea, and Livinstone, Sonia, 'How
    Can Parents Support Children's Internet Safety',
    LSE Research Online, n.d., http://eprints.lse.
    ac.uk/42872/1/How%20can%20parents%20
    support%20children%E2%80%99s%20internet%20
    safety%28lsero%29.pdf. f
2. Media Moms & Digital Dads: A Fact-Not-Fear
    Approach to Parenting in the Digital Age. Uhls, Yalda T.
    Bibliomotion, New York. 2017. Page 52.
3. ScienceDaily, 'Intrusive Monitoring of Internet Use by
    Parents Actually Leads Adolescents to Increase Their
    Risky Online Behavior', January 15, 2015, https://www.
    sciencedaily.com/releases/2015/01/150121093507.htm.
4. The iConnected Parent: Staying Close to Your Kids in
    College (and Beyond) While Letting Them Grow Up.
    Abigail Sullivan Moore and Barbara K. Hofer. Simon and
    Schuster.
5. Manczak, Erika M., Anita DeLongis, and Edith Chen,
    'Does Empathy Have a Cost? Diverging Psychological
    and Physiological Effects within Families', *Health
    Psychology* 35, no. 3 (January 1, 2016): 211–18. https://
    doi.org/10.1037/hea0000281.

Chapter Eight

1. Wikipedia contributors, 'Continuous Partial Attention',
    Wikipedia, April 3, 2023, https://en.wikipedia.org/wiki/
    Continuous_partial_attention.

2. Radesky, Jenny, 'What Happens When We Turn to Smartphones to Escape Our Kids?' *Pacific Standard*, April 18, 2019, https://psmag.com/ideas/what-happens-when-parents-cant-put-their-phones-down.

3. Christakis, Erika, 'Parents' Screen Time Is Hurting Kids', *Atlantic*, February 14, 2022, https://www.theatlantic.com/magazine/archive/2018/07/the-dangers-of-distracted-parenting/561752/.

4. Bowles, Nellie, 'Is the Answer to Phone Addiction a Worse Phone?' *New York Times*, January 19, 2018, https://www.nytimes.com/2018/01/12/technology/grayscale-phone.html.

Chapter Nine

1. Berger, Sarah, 'Tech-Free Dinners and No Smartphones Past 10 Pm—How Steve Jobs, Bill Gates and Mark Cuban Limited Their Kids' Screen Time', CNBC, June 5, 2018, https://www.cnbc.com/2018/06/05/how-bill-gates-mark-cuban-and-others-limit-their-kids-tech-use.html.

2. Bilton, Nick, 'Steve Jobs Was a Low-Tech Parent', *New York Times*, September 10, 2014, https://www.nytimes.com/2014/09/11/fashion/steve-jobs-apple-was-a-low-tech-parent.html?_r=0.

Scan QR code to access the
Penguin Random House India website